SECRE'
WORCEST

Exploring Worcestershire with
10 original tours and unusual places to visit

Irene Boston

S. B. Publications

By the same author:
100 Walks in Warwickshire & West Midlands
Strolls & Walks from Midland Villages
Town & Village Discovery Trails - Warwickshire

First published in 1997 by S.B. Publications
c/o 19 Grove Road, Seaford, East Sussex BN25 1TP

ISBN 1 85770 133 X

Typeset and printed by Island Press Ltd.
3 Cradle Hill Industrial Estate, Seaford, East Sussex BN25 3JE
Telephone: 01323 490222 UK

CONTENTS

	page
Introduction	iv
1. TRANSPORTS OF DELIGHT	1
2. RELICS OF INDUSTRY	9
3. THE LUNGS OF A CITY	19
4. IN A COUNTRY CHURCHYARD	27
5. TO THE WOODS	37
6. COUNTRY SEATS AND COUNTRY GARDENS	45
7. IF MUSIC BE THE FOOD OF LOVE	53
8. CRY HAVOC AND LET SLIP THE DOGS OF WAR	63
9. HOME SWEET HOME	73
10. BLOSSOM BY BLOSSOM THE SPRING BEGINS	83
Tourist Information Centres	90

Front cover: Windmill, Avoncroft Museum of Restored Historic Buildings, Bromsgrove.

Back cover: Cherry blossom, St Faith's churchyard, Overbury, near Bredon Hill.

Title page: Statue of Eve, Spetchley Park Gardens, near Worcester

Line drawings by Elizabeth Francis-Jones

INTRODUCTION

Peaceful, unspoilt Worcestershire has escaped much of the tourist mêlée which afflicts neighbouring Shakespeare's Warwickshire and the Cotswolds. Of course there are popular areas crawling with people during the summer and although it's tempting to bemoan the crowds, it's easy to see why they're drawn to this beautiful county. The income they generate is also an important part of the local economy. But even these "honeypots" are quiet during midweek or out of season. Residents have their own favourite places off the beaten track; fertile river valleys, lush woodland, enchanting villages and rolling hills - all waiting to be explored.

The countryside itself is one of tremendous contrasts. Rising abruptly, the hills of the Malverns, Bredon, Abberley, Clent and the Lickeys form the county's borders. Three major rivers exert a profound influence on the shape of the countryside; some towns and villages owe their very existence to these waterways. The mighty Severn splits the county on its journey to the Severn estuary while the Teme and Avon meander through a rural hinterland. The Industrial Revolution left a legacy of canals, now popular with walkers and cyclists as well as boat users.

The county is dotted with quintessentially English villages with a medley of black and white timber and Georgian elegance. A sprinkling of golden stone reflects its proximity to the Cotswolds. The Vale of Evesham offers some of the richest market gardening in the country, rivalling England's other "garden", Kent. The manufacture of the famous sauce and porcelain have made Worcester a household name. Both Elgar and Housman drew inspiration from the county of their birth.

Strictly speaking, Worcestershire no longer exists. In the early 1970's, it merged with Herefordshire, creating a massive, unwieldy county, little to the liking of either. The proposed future split will be a relief to everyone. We ignore such lunacy and concentrate on the "old" Worcestershire.

Worcestershire is a favourite refuge of mine. I've spent many days touring, either on foot, or in the car, but always with a camera and binoculars and I've grown to love its subtle charm. During such explorations I was conscious that certain areas were linked by common themes, from styles of architecture to events in history. These themes form the backbone of this book.

The ten tours are designed to allow plenty of stops, for you can only explore a town or village properly on foot - scenery through a car window is a poor substitute for Shanks's pony. Where practical, we avoid main roads but the route often depends on the location of bridges over the river Severn. Use common sense on minor roads and *please* keep your speed down; our legal limit is still too fast for these narrow country lanes.

Suitable places for refreshments have been suggested but the list is in no way exhaustive, despite the temptations of a pub crawl - in the interests of research, of course. Remember that places do change hands and therefore menus. Not all the possibilities in towns have been included; little space would be left for anything else.

The sketch maps (not to scale) will give you an overall idea of the route and arrows indicate the direction of travel. Three Ordnance Survey Landranger maps, (nos 138, 139 and 150) cover Worcestershire; they are invaluable for following the directions. Please check opening times of attractions which vary from year to year. A current telephone number is given, although I'm sure BT will change everyone's number again and make these obsolete!

To round off each Tour, I've suggested other areas, still on the same theme, which you may like to explore in the future. I hope this small selection tempts you to wander further afield in this most fascinating of counties.

THE AUTHOR

Irene Boston lives in Warwickshire, having spent her early years in London. As a freelance photographer, she supplies images for postcards, calendars, magazines and books. A keen birdwatcher and naturalist, she enjoys walking, local history and exploring as much of Britain as time will allow. Previous walking books have included two on Warwickshire and another on West Midland villages.

WORCESTERSHIRE
KEY TO TOURS

Kidderminster

1

Bewdley

3

2

Stour Port
on Severn

Bromsgrove

Redditch

Tenbury
Wells

4

Droitwich

5

Worcester

6

7

Malvern

8

Pershore

10

Upton on
Severn

9

Evesham

Bredon

1. TRANSPORTS OF DELIGHT

A trip through northern Worcestershire provides countless reminders of momentous changes in the history of transport. For centuries, the muddy, rutted tracks laughably known as roads meant that it was easier to move goods and people by water. The river Severn was a vital trade link until the canals provided a faster and cheaper way of transporting goods to the industrial centres.

By the 1800's, the days of river trade were fast declining. The railways sounded the final death knell, although the network was slow to arrive in Worcestershire, the first line not opening until 1840. Years later, the efforts of a small band of enthusiasts saved the Kidderminster to Bridgnorth line from Beeching's axe. Today we can enjoy a ride behind a steam train on this Severn Valley Railway, one of the most scenic routes in the country.

The waterways are of immense value to wildlife and increasingly popular with holidaymakers. When the canals were first built, tourists were the last thing on the designers' minds, but nowadays these visitors ensure their survival. The only way to appreciate a canal, short of cruising along it, is to walk its towpaths and although these are not rights of way, walkers are welcome. On our tour we have the perfect opportunity to stop for a stroll along both the river Severn and the Staffordshire and Worcestershire Canal.

TOUR 1 – TRANSPORTS OF DELIGHT

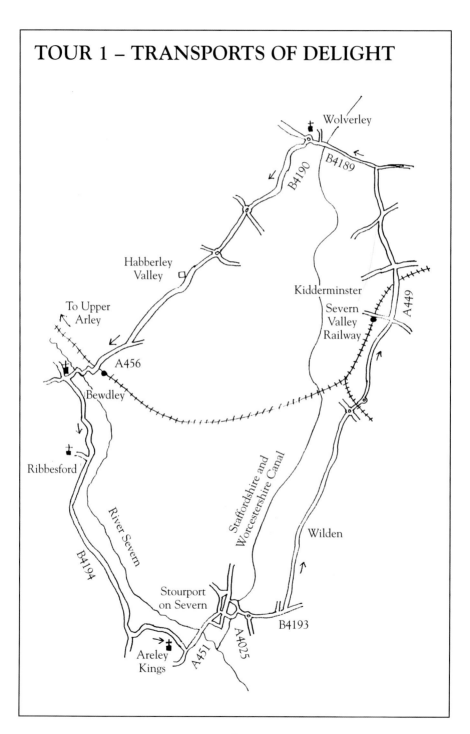

DIRECTIONS:

From the one-way system in Stourport on Severn, join the A4025, signed Worcester and turn left at a roundabout onto B4193, signed Hartlebury. Take second left turn, signed Wilden and church. Follow road for 3 miles to roundabout. Go straight on, signed A449 Wolverhampton and pass under viaduct. At second roundabout, turn left, still on A449. (Signs for Severn Valley Railway appear and the station is left at next traffic lights). Return to traffic lights and turn left, signed A449. Straight over next lights and where road bends right, take minor road on left by Hare & Hounds pub and bus lane sign. Drive steeply uphill and at T-junction, turn left on B4189.

Drop downhill, over canal and past turning to Wolverley village. At next roundabout, turn left on B4190, signed Bewdley. Go straight over next two roundabouts and past turning for Habberley Valley to reach T-junction. Turn right into Bewdley. Follow road over river bridge and up main street, passing left of church on one way system. Just past church, turn left, onto the B4194, Load Street. This road runs under bypass and alongside the Severn. After 2 miles, just past a sharp right bend, look for an unsigned minor road on the left which leads past Areley Kings church to A451. Turn left to return to Stourport.

APPROX. DISTANCE: 16 miles

RECOMMENDED:

Ample choice in Stourport on Severn, Kidderminster and Bewdley; The Rock Tavern, Wilden; The Lock, Queen's Head Inn, Wolverley; The Woodman, Ribbesford.

The natural starting point for our Tour is STOURPORT ON SEVERN, which is proud of its tradition as the only town in the country to be built solely as a consequence of the canal trade. It was once the busiest inland port in the Midlands after Birmingham. Stourport developed at the point where the STAFFORDSHIRE and WORCESTERSHIRE CANAL, built by James Brindley in 1772, joins the river Severn. Within ten years, foundries, tanneries, mills, carpet factories and vinegar works had sprung up, which in turn spawned warehouses, shops, houses and inns, all supporting a considerable local population. The development of the railways caused canal trade to decline, although it is ironic that the railway is now closed and used as a cycle route and walkway while the canal bustles with leisure craft. The distinctive Clock Warehouse in the canal basin, elegant Georgian buildings in the town and the picturesque riverside setting all add to Stourport's charm.

For centuries, Britain's longest river, the SEVERN, was one of four great waterways, along with the Trent, Thames and Ouse, which carried the bulk of Britain's trade. The Severn rises on Plynlimon in the Welsh hills, gathering many streams into its arms before sweeping through Shropshire and Worcestershire to pour into the vast Severn Estuary and the Bristol Channel. The river brought considerable wealth to the region although there has always been a heavy price to pay. Even today, during high tides or

Clock Warehouse, Staffordshire & Worcestershire canal, Stourport on Severn.

following exceptionally heavy rain, land either side of the river floods. Swollen by the winter rains, the formidable power and speed of the river is an awesome sight. In Worcester, riverside streets are submerged, swans glide over the pavements, the cricket ground is inundated and the only activity possible on the racecourse is water polo.

Just about every type of cargo from pottery, salt, corn, coal, cider and even wine was carried on the Severn. Inevitably, other industries grew up to service this trade and locals found employment in boat building, loading goods, and inn keeping. The most common craft was the flat bottomed, twin masted trow. The coracle, a much lighter and far more portable craft, was used mostly for personal journeys.

Today, leisure activities are as important and lucrative as commercial traffic once was. During the summer at Stourport, steamers ply up and down carrying hundreds of tourists. (Tel: 01299 871177 and 01299 822303 for timings). Boat rides are also available at Upton upon Severn and Worcester. The Severn is particularly valuable for wildlife, supporting many breeding species. Migrating birds use the river as the avian equivalent of a motorway on their journey to breeding grounds further north.

We follow roads parallel to the canal and through the industrial outskirts of KIDDERMINSTER, passing under a spectacular viaduct. Visitors

Steam Train, Severn Valley Railway, Upper Arley station.

descend in droves to ride on the SEVERN VALLEY RAILWAY, which hugs the course of the Severn through 16 miles of breathtaking countryside. Volunteers maintain the immaculate stations and run the line, one of the most popular attractions in the area. Regular services of steam hauled and diesel passenger trains run throughout the year and special events, such as Santa Specials, keep the kids, and a few adults, amused. Arley station is currently featured in the TV series "Oh, Doctor Beeching", a fitting irony when you remember that this gentleman very nearly killed off the line. You can buy a reasonably priced "Freedom of the Line" ticket which allows you to get off at any station to explore, returning on a later train. The railway is well placed for walks, both linear along the river and circular from the stations. (Trains run daily, May to September and weekends during winter. Tel: 01299 403816. Talking timetable: 01299 401001).

Victoria Bridge carrying Severn Valley Railway over river Severn, north of Bewdley.

We climb steeply out of Kidderminster and soon have the opportunity to turn aside to visit WOLVERLEY, set amidst enchanting canal and river scenery. The bizarre church looms over the village while sandstone caves, at the rear of the pub, were once inhabited. Sadly, they are now used as a rubbish dump.

After passing through yet more suburbia, we drive, with some relief, into open country to HABBERLEY VALLEY. The acres of heath and woodland combined with high sandstone cliffs are a haven of tranquillity, best appreciated from two waymarked walks.

Unless you were tempted to take the train from Kidderminster, you enter BEWDLEY over Telford's Bridge. The fourth structure at this important crossing, it was built in 1798 by Thomas Telford. Just downstream is the site of previous bridges; the last was constructed in 1483 and survived until floods in 1795 swept it away. The Severn is still crossed by relatively few roads and this waterway continues to dictate any choice of route across the county.

Bewdley's ancient name, "beau lieu" meaning beautiful place, is particularly apt and the town retains an air of individuality with many elegant buildings. The settlement prospered as an inland port, dependent on trade from the river Severn. Wool, coal and wood were transported to Bristol, for onward shipment to Europe.

Unfortunately, or fortunately, if you prefer Bewdley as it is, the canal network bypassed the town. The canal was destined to follow the line of the river Stour to end at a spot further south, which became, as we have seen, Stourport. Consequently, Bewdley's prosperity declined.

Bewdley can boast several notable figures from the past. Three times Prime Minister Stanley Baldwin was born at Lower Park House in 1867. At Tickenhill Manor, Prince Arthur married Catherine of Aragon by proxy in 1499, and Arthur's body rested here on its way to burial at Worcester cathedral. Catherine, of course, later became the first of Henry VIII's marital sextet.

The town has had its share of strange street names. Most intriguing of all was Whispering Street (now Westbourne Street) where fugitives crossed the river by ford or coracle after dark, thus avoiding the bridge guards. St. Anne's church, shaken to its foundations and begrimed by passing traffic, is a central feature in any view from the bridge. Bewdley Museum is also worth a visit. (Open Easter to September, Weds-Fri 10.30-4.30, Weekends & Bank Holidays 12.-5.00. Tel: 01299 403573).

If you have time, follow a delightful riverside footpath upstream to Upper Arley, returning down the opposite bank, or by train. A walk will do you more good if you've been tempted into Upper Arley's tea shop!

Our route out of Bewdley passes under the new bypass. Sadly, Worcestershire has not escaped the invasion of the car. Most towns and some villages are now bypassed, although those same residents who campaign for a new road, inevitably end up complaining about the noise it generates. Enjoy Worcestershire while you can before it disappears under tarmac.

The road runs past RIBBESFORD church which has many interesting features including 15th century carvings, mediaeval glass and a 13th century bell, said to be the oldest in Worcestershire. Ribbesford Woods, overlooking the river from the heights of Stagborough Hill, are a pleasure to walk through, away from traffic and the noise of civilisation. We return to Stourport along minor roads passing Areley Kings church.

FURTHER EXPLORATION:

WORCESTER AND BIRMINGHAM CANAL was built to provide a link for the porcelain industry with the rest of the canal network. After years of construction problems, it finally opened in 1815. The 36 locks of TARDEBIGGE FLIGHT, which raise the canal over 200 feet in $2^{1}/_{2}$ miles, represent a remarkable engineering achievement; a feat which may be lost on the sweating holidaymakers toiling up and down them each summer. It's an enjoyable spectactor sport and you may even be roped in to help - if you're unlucky!

On TOUR 2 we pass by the DROITWICH CANAL.

2. RELICS OF INDUSTRY

Worcestershire can lay claim to a rich industrial heritage and the whole area is resonant with connections to past and present commercial endeavours. Coal and iron deposits north of the Clent Hills were centred on Dudley, now in the West Midlands. Activities as diverse as salt extraction, the making of scythes, carpets, porcelain and needles once formed the backbone of the local economy. Our tour starts in Droitwich where the abundant salt deposits, left over from the time Worcestershire was on the sea bed, have been mined for almost 2,000 years. John Corbett, the "Salt King" was responsible for the development of Droitwich as a spa resort. Visitors are still attracted to the town to sample its therapeutic waters.

The fascinating Avoncroft Museum in Bromsgrove houses a unique collection of buildings rescued from destruction which span seven centuries. The mill villages of Belbroughton and Blakedown bear testimony to the importance of scythe making, cornmills and ironworks. The tranquillity of these villages is a far cry from the noise, filth and hardship of foundry life. The only legacy of the mills in Belbroughton is the use of old millstones as unusual cottage steps, garden walls or in the stream bed.

Ancient salt roads, used to convey goods by packhorse, can still be traced today. The Worcester to Birmingham A38 and the Droitwich to Alcester B4090 closely follow the line of old Roman roads.

We return through Kidderminster, for so long the heart of Britain's carpet making industry. No one could pretend that these towns at the southern tip of the West Midlands are the most attractive in the county, but their local history and industrial archaeology are absorbing and intriguing.

TOUR 2 – RELICS OF INDUSTRY

Blakedown   A450

B4188

Kidderminster   A456   A491

Town
Centre   Belbroughton

Fairfield

M5

Catshill

A449

M42/M5
Interchange

A442

A450   B4091   Museum

Bromsgrove   A44

A38

Avoncroft
Museum

A38   Roman Road

Droitwich

B4090 Saltway

DIRECTIONS:

Leave Droitwich on the A38 north, and at the roundabout on the outskirts of Bromsgrove, turn right, still on the A38, to the Avoncroft Museum. After your visit, turn right on the A38 and at the second roundabout, turn left into Bromsgrove. Leave the town on the B4091, which you follow through Catshill, straight over a mini roundabout and through Fairfield to another roundabout. Turn left onto the A491 (dual carriageway) and in just over a mile, turn left onto the B4188 to Belbroughton.

At the T-junction in the village, turn left and follow signs to Blakedown to a crossroads on the A450. Go straight across, still on the B4188 into Blakedown. Turn left on the dual A456 to Kidderminster. Following your visit, join the A449 south, signed Worcester. After nearly 3 miles, go left on A442 and straight over a roundabout, still on the A442, back to Droitwich.

APPROX. DISTANCE: 34 miles

RECOMMENDED:

Plenty of choice in Droitwich, Bromsgrove and Kidderminster; The Swan, The Crown, Wychbold; The Talbot, Ye Olde Horseshoe, The Queens, Belbroughton; The Swan, The Old House at Home, Blakedown.

DROITWICH's prosperity is founded upon salt and during Roman times it was known as Salinae, "the place of salt". Richard, Droitwich's patron saint who later became Bishop of Chichester, is remembered for a miracle in 1250 when the brine failed and was restored only after he blessed the pit. However, it was largely through the efforts of John Corbett that Droitwich developed into a fashionable Victorian spa. We can be thankful to men like Corbett for making salt an affordable commodity, rather than the luxury item it was then. Salt mining ended in the 19th century but visitors can

Statue of St. Richard & St. Augustine's church, Droitwich.

still enjoy the brine pool. The incredibly salty water is ten times stronger than sea water, similar to the Dead Sea, although before punters are pickled in it, the water is diluted to sea water strength. (Spa baths open all year. Mon-Fri 11.30-8.30, Weekends 10.00-4.00. Sessions must be booked. Tel: 01905 794894). A visit to the Heritage Centre next door is a must. (Open Mon-Fri, 9.30-5.00 in summer, 9.30-4.30-winter, Sat 10.00-4.00. Free admission. Tel: 01905 774312). Corbett was responsible for many of the town's buildings, the most spectacular example was his own home, Chateau Impney. Resembling a French chateau, it is now, more mundanely, a hotel.

The Droitwich Canal was built by James Brindley in 1771 to serve the salt trade. The section through Droitwich still contains water but further

Heritage Centre, Droitwich.

south in the Salwarpe valley, the canal is "dry". Enthusiasts are restoring the neglected section, and whilst we hope they succeed, this dereliction has brought positive benefits. Wildlife is quick to colonise a disused canal and among the reed-beds you may be lucky enough to glimpse sedge and reed warblers, summer visitors who breed in this wetland habitat. If this was a fast flowing waterway, busy with canal boats, these birds would not be here.

On the outskirts of Bromsgrove, the AVONCROFT MUSEUM is devoted to a collection, taken from all over the country, of buildings rescued from destruction. Stand in awe beneath one of its chief treasures, the original roof of Guesten Hall from Worcester Cathedral, the sheer beauty and intricate detail of its timbers transcends the

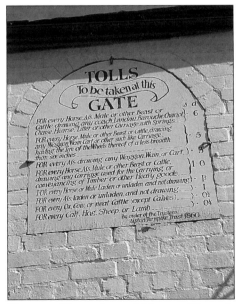

Plaque on toll house, Avoncroft Museum of Restored Historic Buildings, Bromsgrove.

modern brick building it now covers. What brings this museum to life is the masterstroke of making it a working museum with regular demonstrations in the craft of brickmaking, blacksmith, woodturning, chainmaking and racksawing. The museum also houses the National Telephone Kiosk Collection. (Open Tues-Thurs, weekends, March & November, 10.30-4.00. April/May and Sept/Oct, daily except Mon, 10.30-4.30. June / August, daily, 10.30-5.00. Admission charge. Tel: 01527 831886/831363)

We continue into Bromsgrove, a bustling town with a rich history but sadly, much

Telephone Kiosk Collection, Avoncroft Museum of Historic Buildings, Bromsgrove.

arid modern development. A.E. Housman once lived here and his statue can be seen in the main centre, somewhat incongruously set amid shops and crowds. Worth a visit is the BROMSGROVE MUSEUM with displays of local industry and crafts. (Open all year. Mon-Sat 9.30-5.00, Sun 2.00-5.00. Admission charge. Tel: 01527 577983). In the churchyard of St. John the Baptist, seek out the highly distinctive graves of Thomas Scaife and Joseph Rutherford, killed when the boiler of the steam engine they were driving blew up on the notorious Lickey incline.

We drive out through quieter countryside to BELBROUGHTON, once a scythe making centre of excellence. For over 400 years, scythes made here were in demand around the world and the last factory only closed in 1967. During the height of the industry eleven pubs served the needs of the thirsty workforce. Take a look at the old plating hammer and millstones on the village green. Holy Trinity church is also worth a visit.

Old plating hammer, village green, Belbroughton.

Our next stop is BLAKEDOWN, just off the main road in the midst of a pleasantly wooded district dotted with lakes, which were dammed to provide power for cornmills and ironworks. The present aura of peace and tranquillity is popular with fishermen, walkers and birds. Originally, the village lay on the route of the saltway and the later arrival of the railway increased the area's prosperity.

We passed through KIDDERMINSTER on Tour 1, but return now wearing a different hat. To appreciate the many features of interest you must explore on foot. There is no doubting the town's antiquity, which probably dates back to the 7th century when it was a centre for missionaries. The name may come from Cydda, possibly the name of a Saxon, combined with minster, unsurprisingly a Saxon word for church or monastery. Cloth weaving became important in the 13th century with carpets taking over from the 1700's. In the 19th century, the development of carpet power looms meant that Kidderminster became the most important centre in the country. It declined dramatically in the 1980's, although the town still

Statue of Rowland Hill, Inventor of Penny Post, Kidderminster.

retains a significant position in the industry. Brintons Carpet Factory was established in 1783. Memorials to the more prominent manufacturers can be found in the parish church while mill buildings remain as testimony to the town's heritage.

Along the stretch of the Staffordshire and Worcestershire Canal which winds through the town were sited four wharves serving an iron foundry, the cloth and carpet trade and a flour mill. The latter had its own railway track through the site now occupied by Sainsbury's.

Sir Rowland Hill, creator of the Penny Post in 1840, was born here and his statue stands in the town. An intriguing story concerns the building of St. Mary's. Originally supposed to be built elsewhere, each night the stones were moved by mysterious forces and placed on the present site. The builders eventually gave up and built the church where the mischief makers, said to be angels, decreed. Whatever the truth of the story, on the tower can be seen angels, obviously training as hod carriers, holding a segment of an arch. Near the church is the statue of Richard Baxter, a 17th century non-conformist minister who wielded enormous influence in the town. The carved sanctuary screen depicts various local activities including sheep shearing, ploughing and carpet making. The delicate Whittall Chapel houses stained glass showing three women of courage, Florence Nightingale, Saint Mary and Joan of Arc.

FURTHER EXPLORATION:

It was once said that REDDITCH "standeth among needles and fish hooks", which conjures up a very uncomfortable picture but was nevertheless true. Prospering during the Industrial Revolution, it became the needle making capital of the world with 90% of the world's needles produced here. The Forge Mill Needle Museum is housed in the original 18th century mill building which operated until the 1960's. (Open April to Sept, Mon-Thurs 11.00-4.30, Weekends 2.00-5.00. Restricted winter opening, closed January. Admission charge. Tel: 01527 62509). Sharing the same site is Bordesley Abbey (TOUR 6).

We visit the JINNEY RING CRAFT CENTRE, Hanbury on TOUR 6. The ROYAL WORCESTER PORCELAIN factory in Worcester houses the Dyson Perrins Museum and the largest collection of Royal Worcester porcelain in the world. Visitors can tour the workshops and pick up bargains in the factory shop. (Open Mon-Sat 10.00-5.00. Factory tours Mon-Fri starting at 10.25 but no children under 11 and the stairs make the tour unsuitable for the infirm. Admission charge. Tel: 01905 23221)

HARTLEBURY COUNTY MUSEUM holds various exhibitions and craft demonstrations throughout the year on subjects as diverse as advertising, transport and bloomers - that's the passion killers not the flowering variety! (Open daily except Sat. March to November. Mon-Thurs 10.00-5.00, Fri & Sun 2.00-5.00, Bank Holidays 11.00-5.00. Admission charge. Tel: 01299 250416).

The Worcester Royal Porcelain Works.

3. THE LUNGS OF A CITY

Three Worcestershire Country Parks rub shoulders with the edge of the West Midlands conurbation forming Birmingham's own green belt. Their survival is all the more remarkable considering their proximity to this concrete jungle. They are all extremely popular with people who appreciate such open spaces on their doorstep.

Pockets of countryside near urban areas are particularly vulnerable to development and some form of protection is vital. Designating these fragile sites as nature reserves, Country Parks, or SSSI's is often the only way to ensure their survival. The local council and voluntary organisations work extremely hard to safeguard these valuable havens. Even this protection can be illusory and no site is immune from destruction when yet another bypass or industrial estate is deemed necessary.

The term "Country Park" is almost a misnomer. These are not theme parks or zoos where wildlife performs to order. The skills and patience you will need to observe wildlife are the same as in the remotest countryside. Most parks have a visitor centre offering a selection of leaflets, while rangers organise guided walks throughout the year.

The first thing to do when you arrive at all these Country Parks, is to get rid of the car and walk; so pack your walking boots or trainers. Paths abound and you can generally wander at will. If you have a choice, avoid Bank Holiday weekends - it's likely that everyone else has had the same idea and by their very presence, destroy the peace and quiet they seek. In winter, when the weather discourages many visitors or during mid week: these are times to savour Country Parks.

TOUR 3 – THE LUNGS OF A CITY

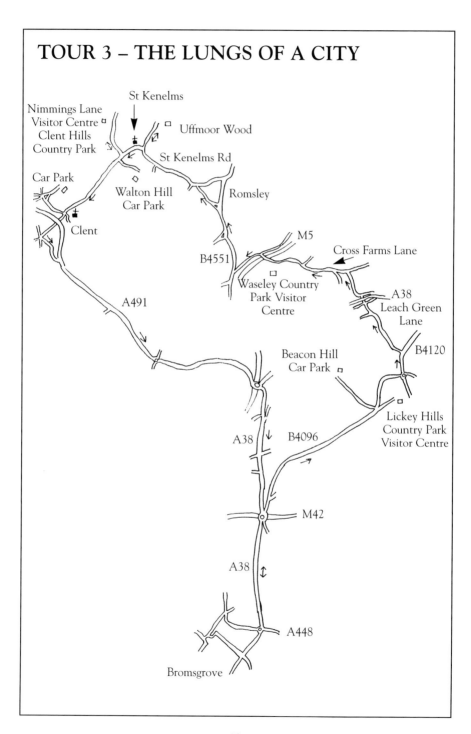

DIRECTIONS:

From Bromsgrove, take A38 north to M42 roundabout. Take third exit, signed Rednall on B4096. After 3 miles, reach right turn to Lickey Hills Visitor Centre. Return to junction, turn right downhill on B4096 to roundabout and left on B4120. Just after road becomes dual, turn left down Leach Green Lane. After a mile, reach junction under A38 dual carriageway. Go straight across to another T-junction and turn left. The road climbs past estates to T-junction. Turn left onto Cross Farms Lane and in just under 2 miles, reach entrance to Waseley Country Park.

After visiting, return to junction, turn left over M5 and follow road as it bends left on Old House Lane. At T-junction, turn right on B4551. As road descends into Romsley, take second left, Poplar Lane. At T-junction, turn left onto St. Kenelms Road, signed Clent. In just over a mile, bear right downhill to Uffmoor Wood. After visiting, turn left uphill and first right, signed Clent Village past St. Kenelm's church. Take first right to Clent Hills Visitor Centre. From car park entrance, turn right and at T-junction, right again downhill past Clent church and straight over junction onto Church Avenue. Go under A491 to T-junction. Turn left to major junction. Turn right, with care, onto A491 and follow signs back to Bromsgrove.

APPROX. DISTANCE: 20 miles

RECOMMENDED:

Visitor Centre Café, Lickey Hills; Poachers Pocket, Lickey roundabout; Café, Waseley Country Park; Refreshments, Nimmings Lane Visitor Centre, Clent Hills; The Vine Inn, The Bell & Cross, Clent village.

We leave Bromsgrove and climb steeply into open country to the LICKEY HILLS COUNTRY PARK visitor centre. Created a country park in 1971 to prevent further encroachment from surrounding surburbia, this blend of deciduous woodland, conifer plantations, heathland and ornamental gardens is a nature lover's paradise. An enormous debt of gratitude is owed to the Cadbury family who rescued large areas of countryside from developers. Their generosity is commemorated by a stone fountain. On Beacon Hill, near a modern stone "fort", picnickers on the grassy slopes revel in exhilarating views across the Black Country. You can link both parts of the park on foot but care is needed when crossing the busy road slicing through the middle.

Walker, Beacon fort, Lickey Hills.

The diverse habitat supports a tremendous range of wildlife. Breeding birds include redstart, tree pipit and redpoll. During winter, many birds band together for protection. Listen for their calls as the flock moves through the woodland foraging for food. Beech mast provides essential food for chaffinches and tits, while holly bushes produce a valuable crop of berries which support fieldfares, thrushes and redwings through harsh winters. Although it's easy to be critical of conifer plantations, they provide a precious sanctuary for birds such as goldcrest, siskins, coal tits and crossbills which thrive in these specialised habitats.

Gate, North Worcester Path, Waseley Hills Country Park.

If you can tear yourself away, our next stop is WASELEY COUNTRY PARK. Until the 16th century, Waseley belonged to Chadwich Manor. Centuries later, the Cadbury family bought the land and donated it to the National Trust. Waseley is almost surrounded in a pincer movement by the ugly intrusion of the M5 and houses, factories and roads crowding its northern edge. From the visitor centre, you can climb to Windmill Hill where the fascinating vista includes the Black Country to the north and the glorious sweep of the Malverns and Cotswolds further south. Considering how close you are to surburbia, a marvellous panorama of woodland and open country is revealed. The pasture, gorse and woodland are home to a splendid variety of wildlife and flowers.

All three parks are linked by the North Worcestershire Path, a mini long distance footpath of 27 miles which skirts the edge of the West Midlands but still manages to retain a pleasantly rural flavour.

After crossing the M5, you enter an incredible area of open space, with well marked footpaths. You soon reach UFFMOOR WOOD, a place of secluded dingles, trickling streams, broadleaved trees and a scrubby understorey. A small car park in Uffmoor Lane allows access to a network of paths. The open rides, used as hunting corridors by birds of prey and owls, are also invaluable for wildflowers and butterflies. Glimpses of Halesowen through the trees show how perilously close the urban fringe is. For many years Uffmoor was closed to the public but passed into the safe hands of the Woodland Trust in 1986 where open access for future generations is assured. The Trust's aim of protecting our woodlands is achieved with enormous effort and limited resources. (Membership details from Autumn Park, Grantham, Lincs NG31 6Ll. Tel: 01476 74297)

A narrow road leads to the simple, unassuming ST. KENELM'S CHURCH, sheltering below the Clent Hills. The church is associated with a sad and tragic tale from the 9th century. King Kenelm, little more than a

Walker, Uffmoor Wood, nr Clent Hills.

child, was murdered on the orders of his ambitious sister. At the scene of the crime, a spring is believed to have gushed forth and a church was later built on the site. Recent renovations below the churchyard have restored the spring and over the lychgate is a carving of the boy king, a rather pathetic figure. Inside the church, leaflets relate the full dramatic story which contains enough incident to rival anything on television.

A short drive away is the Nimmings Lane car park of the CLENT HILLS COUNTRY PARK. These hills attract nearly a million visitors a year, although the majority of visitors venture only a short distance from their cars. If you are prepared to walk, you can easily get away from the crowds. A million people means an awful lot of feet, so it's hardly surprising that erosion is a major problem, and paths across Adam's Hill are fenced off to allow the vegetation to recover. Please do your bit by keeping to the paths and avoiding the grassy edges. A path suitable for wheelchairs leads from the car park to a viewpoint where you can enjoy astonishing views of tremendous contrast. A toposcope helps to identify distant hills. On the summit are the Four Stones; they are not prehistoric but were erected by Lord Lyttleton of nearby Hagley Hall in the 18th century. The graffiti is not the handiwork of his lordship but one of our modern insanities. From here, you can look across Clatterbach valley to the neighbouring ridge of Walton Hill, which repays the effort of climbing it with glorious views. In fact, there

Four Stones in winter, Clent Hills.

is no higher ground to the east until you reach the Urals and it's easy to believe that's just where the icy east wind is blowing from.

A circuit of both hills on a clear day is especially rewarding. Naturalists, particularly birdwatchers, will find much of interest. The open hillside, gorse scrub and woodland provide food and shelter for a variety of birds. During summer, whitethroats sing their scratchy song on the gorse bushes and yellowhammers warble about "a little bit of bread and no cheese". In winter, flocks of redpolls and siskins search for food in the woods. Each spring and autumn, many birds use these hills as an overnight B & B, resting and refuelling for the next leg of their amazing journeys. You may be lucky and see rare birds such as ring ouzels, similar to a large blackbird but with a white breast band. A small herd of fallow deer wander in from Hagley Hall park and can be found on the lower slopes or in the woodland.

Our route continues through the village of CLENT which has its share of modern housing, although old Clent is full of character and individuality. A stream tumbles alongside the street and attractive cottages cluster around the church.

FURTHER EXPLORATION:

WORCESTER WOODS COUNTRY PARK just outside the city, and signed "Countryside Centre" from most roads, comprises over 100 acres of wildflower meadows and woodland. (Visitor Centre and café. Tel: 01905 766493).

ARROW VALLEY LAKE AND COUNTRY PARK, REDDITCH. 900 acres where you can enjoy walking, boating and fishing. (Tel: 01527 68337).

KINGSFORD COUNTRY PARK, adjacent to Kinver Edge, offers 200 acres of heathland and conifer woodland. Magnificent views and abundant birdlife are a particular feature. (Tel: 01562 710025).

LEAPGATE COUNTRY PARK, part of HARTLEBURY COMMON, is a precious remnant of heathland, a unique habitat that deserves protection. It's one of the few areas in the Midlands where you can walk across shifting sand dunes and discover Worcestershire's only acid bog. In the 19th century, sand and gravel were extracted and hippopotamus bones were discovered, but you won't meet such exotic inhabitants today. It's more likely you'll encounter woodland and heath birds, such as meadow pipits, stonechats and several species of warbler. (Tel: 01905 766493). Leaflets for these and other Worcestershire Country Parks are available from the Countryside Service on 01562 710025.

4. IN A COUNTRY CHURCHYARD

Church architecture has changed enormously over the centuries. Little Saxon carving survives as most churches were rebuilt by the Normans. Dominant styles known as Early English and Decorated were followed by striking examples from the Perpendicular period. A particular feature of Worcestershire churches is the amount of wood, a legacy of the days when great swathes of forest covered the county. Timber was also used inside, with wooden roofs and galleries much in evidence. Worcestershire is without rival in its Norman architecture, from the great religious houses to humble parish churches.

By the 11th century, the wealth and power enjoyed by the church was enormous, the rich, fertile soil made the Bishop's estates the sixth wealthiest in the land. Only the priories of Worcester, Great Malvern and Halesowen (now in the West Midlands), together with the abbeys at Evesham and Pershore survived the purge of the Dissolution. Later, the Reformation halted all new building, work only restarting after the Restoration of Charles II. The Baroque style became fashionable, eventually replaced by Gothic. The Victorians' mania for restoration ripped the heart out of many churches; their habit of scraping walls bare destroyed countless paintings.

Our tour, starting from Tenbury Wells, visits a small fraction of the county's fascinating places of worship, from the unassuming church at Hanley William to Great Witley, whose baroque splendour is without equal. Take your binoculars to relish details of distant carvings and wonder at the skill and sense of humour of long vanished craftsmen. This ornate work remains their testimony. Please give generously when you visit these churches as the cost of maintenance is way beyond the purses of the small parishes they serve. Every little helps.

TOUR 4 – IN A COUNTRY CHURCHYARD

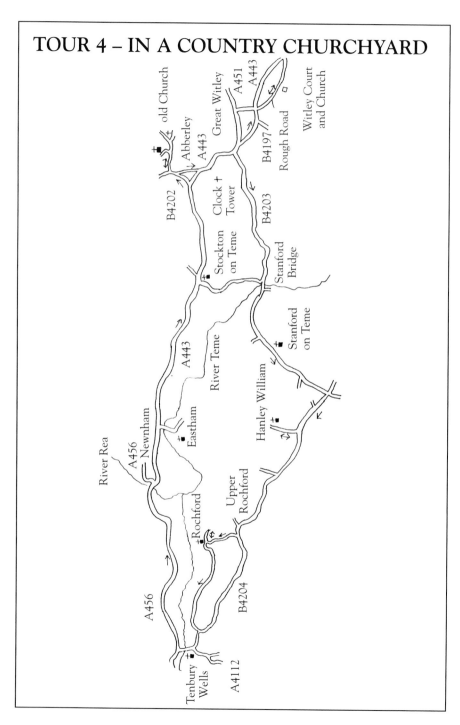

DIRECTIONS:

Starting from Tenbury Wells, cross the bridge over river Teme and turn right on A456. Go through Newnham, ignore left turn to Bewdley and continue on A443, signed Worcester. Pass through Stockton on Teme and after 2 miles, turn left onto B4202, signed Abberley village. At T-junction, turn left and immediately right to visit Abberley. Return to B4202 and turn left, and left again on reaching A443. Drive through Great Witley and look for turning on right, signed Witley Court. (This road is extremely rough, and it's over a mile to the Court. The turning 2 miles further on is equally rough but shorter).

Return to A443 and turn left. Turn left onto B4203, signed Stanford Bridge. The road drops down to cross the bridge and climbs to a crossroads. Turn right on B4204, signed Tenbury Wells. After 2 miles, turn right to Hanley William church. Return to B4204, and turn right to reach Upper Rochford. Just after sharp left bend in the village, turn right on narrow, muddy road. Turn right at T-junction and follow signs to Rochford church. (Small parking area beyond farmyard). Return to junction and turn right, continue straight on at previous junction and follow narrow road to its junction with B4204. Turn right into Tenbury Wells.

APPROX. DISTANCE: 30 miles

RECOMMENDED:

Plenty of pubs and tea shops in Tenbury Wells; Peacock Inn, A456; Talbot Inn, Newnham; Nag's Head, Lindridge; The Manor Arms, Abberley; Hundred House Hotel, Great Witley; Tea Rooms, Witley Court; The Fox Inn, Hanley William; Tally Ho Inn, Broad Heath.

St. Mary's church and friendly village cat(!), Tenbury Wells.

Before you leave TENBURY WELLS, take time to explore. Known as "the town in the orchard", Tenbury's rural setting is enhanced by its position on the banks of the river Teme. Following the discovery of mineral springs in 1839, a Pump Room and Baths were built, but ambitions to develop the town as a fashionable spa never came to fruition. The Pump Room closed in 1939. On entering, one is immediately struck by the size of St. Mary's Church, and the lavish use of timber in the roof and gallery. Two stone effigies are quaintly, and aptly, called Big and Little Crusader and, protected by a glass case, there is a rare fragment of a Saxon cross. A plaque by the chancel is a reminder of a devastating flood in the 18th century when the church was almost overwhelmed by the river.

Our tour runs parallel with the RIVER TEME on both legs of the journey. The river rises in the hills of mid Wales and enters Worcestershire at Tenbury Wells. Fed by Ledwyche Brook, the river Rea and Leigh Brook, the Teme joins the Severn at Worcester near the site of the famous Battle (TOUR 8). Timeless stretches of river valley, untouched by industry, make this one of our most enchanting waterways. The Teme valley, with its characteristic hopyards and orchards, has escaped the worst ravages of intensive farming and the scenery is a revelation. A patchwork of wooded hillsides, lush river valleys, and glory be, *small* fertile fields, with healthy hedgerows full of wildflowers. Not a flail mower in sight.

We pass close to the hamlet of EASTHAM, at the heart of the valley's hop country. Worth a detour over the river bridge is the church of St. Peter and St. Paul, of charming simplicity, with richly carved panelling and a leper window in the chancel.

Nudging the road is the simple church of St. Andrew's at STOCKTON ON TEME. The 14th century porch is a charming miniature version of the nave roof. ABBERLEY clock tower has been clearly visible for some distance. It was designed by the Victorian architect, St. Aubyn, for Joseph Jones and became known as Jones's Folly. Among the many stories surrounding its origins, one in particular appeals. It was built so he could look down on his neighbours at the much grander Witley Court - a matter of the Jones's keeping up with everyone else for a change! The tower dominates the grounds of Abberley Hall, now a private boys' school which can boast Geoffrey Howe and Anthony Quayle among its former pupils.

Abberley village lies below the tree clad Abberley Hill in a glorious setting. A special atmosphere pervades the old Norman church of St. Michael's. By 1850, decay and neglect had left the building almost in ruins. This precarious state continued until the 1960's when villagers raised

Ruined Norman church of St. Michael's, Abberley.

Witley Court.

enough money to salvage the chapel. During this restoration, unique 14th century silver spoons were found buried in the walls. They are now stored in the British Museum but you can see replicas in the Hartlebury County Museum. The chancel is understandably popular for christenings and the grassed churchyard and ruin of the nave are calm and restful. The modern St. Mary's was built to replace the dilapidated old church.

An awful, potholed road leads to WITLEY COURT, a spectacular ruin of a once grand country house. The Dudley family used their fortune, amassed in the industrial revolution, to transform the house into a palatial mansion. Elegant parties and gatherings of the aristocracy and royalty, including Edward VII, were the norm until a disastrous fire in 1937. Years of theft and neglect accelerated the process of decay, leaving the shell you see today. English Heritage have undertaken the huge task of making the ruins safe and accessible to visitors. In the grounds, the colossal Perseus fountain is being restored and gushes on selected days during the summer - water board drought restrictions permitting! The ruins, with their remarkable haunting atmosphere, remain an architectural monument of great splendour and are a haven of peace and tranquillity away from the crowds. They've always been a particular favourite of mine and I'm sure the appalling state of the access road deters many visitors. The guidebook contains fascinating photographs of the court's lavish interior in its heyday. (Open daily April to October 10.00-6.00, Weds-Sun November to March 10.00-4.00. Admission charge, free to English Heritage members. Tel: 01299 896636).

Don't miss GREAT WITLEY CHURCH next door. The plain exterior doesn't prepare you for the glory of the interior. The golden cupola perched on the roof and the doors, which make you feel quite Lilliputian, are perhaps the only clues to anything unusual. Lavishly Roccoco in design, the interior glows with light. The ceiling paintings by Antonio Bellucci, the Joshua Price windows, and Bagutti plasterwork have transformed this humble church into a wonderland of gold and white.

Bump your way back to the main road, drop steeply to cross Stanford Bridge and rise equally sharply to HANLEY WILLIAM. All Saints Church, of striking simplicity, stands in an idyllic setting with superb views north to Clee Hill. The timber turret and shingled spire are particularly distinctive features and in spring, snowdrops add a splash of colour to the tiny churchyard.

ROCHFORD owes its name to its position on the river Teme, where a ford allowed access to the opposite bank. Further evidence of the settlement's antiquity can be seen in the remains of a grass motte, the only

Interior of Great Witley parish church, next to Witley Court.

All Saints church and snowdrops in churchyard, Hanley William, Teme Valley.

sign of a timber fort which defended this ancient ford. Above the fine Norman doorway of St. Michael's Church can be seen a Tree of Life carving on the tympanum, unique in Worcestershire, but suffering the effects of wind and weather. The east window by William Morris is full of beauty and majesty and the churchyard is graced with a sea of white snowdrops in early spring.

FURTHER EXPLORATION:

Take your pick! There is something of interest in almost every Worcestershire church but these are a few to choose from near the Teme valley. St. Mary's, KYRE WYARD (grid ref, 626636) stands within the grounds of the Kyre estate. The spire of St. Peter's, STOKE BLISS (652628) dominates the village. The church at CLIFTON UPON TEME (715615) has a rare dedication to St. Kenelm, a familiar name from TOUR 3.

Although further afield, we cannot ignore the grandest of them all, WORCESTER CATHEDRAL, a truly magnificent structure in a majestic setting, best appreciated from the opposite riverbank. Among its imposing array of treasures are King John's tomb, the crypt, chapter house and mediaeval cloisters. Prince Arthur, the elder brother of Henry VIII, is buried here. Reflect for a moment how different our history would have been had Arthur survived to rule instead of Henry, who was to have been merely Archbishop of Canterbury - ironic when you consider his later difficulties with the church. Amid all this grandeur don't miss the homelier details - buy the guidebook to see everything. The acclaimed Three Choirs Festival is held here every third year. (Open daily 8.00-6.00. No admission charge but visitors are invited to make a donation. Tel: 01905 28854).

5. TO THE WOODS

England was once blanketed by the ancient "wildwood". Only fragments now survive, although Worcestershire retains a heartening amount of tree cover. Privileged glimpses of wildlife are highlights of any woodland walk. Shadowy forms of deer slip through the trees, foxes slink purposefully along the forest margins and butterflies patrol the pathways. Spring is the most joyous time of year when flowers carpet the forest floor and birdsong fills the air. To hear the dawn chorus in the depths of a wood is to experience a wonder of nature.

Each season sees a breathtaking change in flora. Pungent swathes of wild garlic, dainty wood anemones and carpets of bluebells provide a spectacular spring display. Autumn glows with colour and hoar frost coats the tree branches as the stillness of a winter's hibernation descends over the wood.

Studying nature is an immensely satisfying hobby and a great way of introducing children to the countryside. Binoculars and pocket identification books on birds, flowers and trees add immeasurably to your enjoyment. Learning bird calls is extremely useful, particularly in spring and summer when birds hide so easily among the canopy. At least if you know their songs, you'll know what to look for and there are excellent audio tapes and CD's around to get you started.

All wildlife is wary and elusive, with hearing and eyesight far superior to ours. Stand against a tree to break up your outline, keep quiet for a few minutes while the birds become used to your presence and you may be rewarded with close views. Wear subdued colours; a group of brightly coloured blobs crashing through the undergrowth, eyes on the ground and talking loudly won't see a thing. Happy wandering!

TOUR 5 – TO THE WOODS

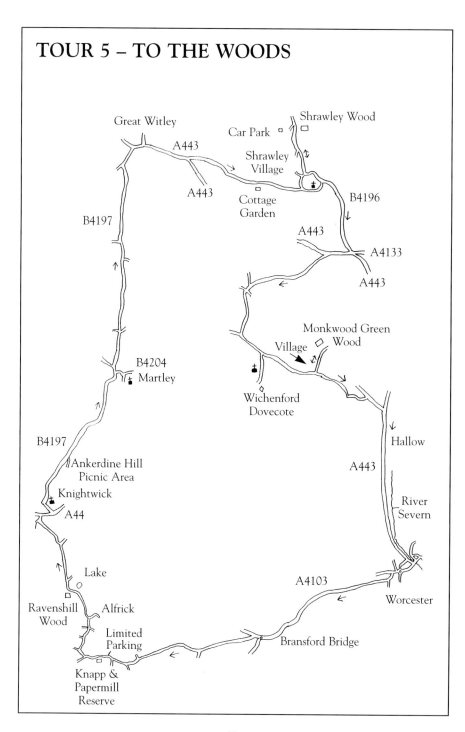

DIRECTIONS:

Leave Worcester on A4103, Hereford road and after Bransford Bridge, turn right at a roundabout, signed Leigh. Keep left when road forks and after 3 miles, as road crosses Leigh Brook, there's limited parking on right for Knapp & Papermill reserve. Continue on road, take first right, signed Alfrick. Keep bearing right, go straight over crossroads to T-junction and turn left. In just over a mile, reach Ravenshill Wood on left, opposite small lake. Continue north, ignoring any side roads, to T-junction at Knightwick. Turn right and right again on A44 and immediately over bridge, left on B4197, signed Martley. Climb Ankerdine Hill and at sharp left bend, unsigned rough road on right leads through houses to picnic area. Continue through Martley to turn right on B4197, signed Stourport and Great Witley.

At T-junction, turn right on A443. After a mile, turn left on minor road, signed Shrawley, which leads past church to village. Turn left on B4196 to visit Shrawley Wood (parking area behind New Inn). Return down B4196 to A4133. Turn right onto A443 and take first left, signed Ockeridge. Go straight over crossroads, following signs to Wichenford. After 2 miles, turn right to church and dovecote. Return to junction, and turn right to Monkwood Green village. By junction on green, turn left, signed Sinton Green to Monkwood Green car park. Return to junction and turn left, signed Hallow. At T-junction, turn right and after 1 mile reach A443. Turn right to return to Worcester.

APPROX. DISTANCE: 36 miles

RECOMMENDED:

The Swan, Alfrick; Fox & Hounds, Ravenhills Green; The Talbot, Knightwick; Admiral Rodney, Berrow Green; The Crown, Martley; Rose & Crown, New Inn, Shrawley.

Leigh Brook running through Knapp & Papermill Nature Reserve.

Our first stop is the KNAPP and PAPERMILL RESERVE, cared for by the Worcestershire Wildlife Trust. The wildflower meadows, steep sided woodland, apple orchards and meandering brook represent a glorious microcosm of the Worcestershire countryside. A place for quiet enjoyment, this peaceful, hidden valley is a precious gem which deserves to be treated with respect. Collect a nature trail leaflet from the warden's house and follow a path past the hide overlooking a bank where kingfishers breed. Butterflies are plentiful, over thirty species having been recorded, including holly blue, dingy skipper and white admiral. Plant life is rich; meadowsweet and common spotted orchids abound. Grey wagtails and dippers bob along the brook while flocks of siskins and long tailed tits comb the woodland for food. Pied flycatchers benefit from the provision of artificial nest boxes. Drifts of bluebells bear testimony to the success of the coppicing programme in clearing patches of woodland to allow light to reach the understorey and wildflowers to regenerate. Picnics are not allowed and dogs must be on leads - both could do irreparable damage to the wildflowers. The Trust performs miracles with very limited funds, so if you care about the wildlife and countryside of your home county, or are a visitor to the area, please consider becoming a member. Or join your local Trust - every county has one. (Entrance free to Trust members, donations requested from everyone else. Details of Worcestershire Wildlife Trust membership from Lower Smite Farm, Smite Hill, Hindlip, Worcester WR3 8SZ. Tel: 014905 754919.)

Primroses, Knapp & Papermill Nature Reserve.

Continue through the outskirts of the charming village of Alfrick to reach RAVENSHILL WOOD, managed by the local Wildlife Trust but privately owned. People are welcome but are asked to respect this privilege for the sake of future generations. Leaflets, detailing two nature trails, are available from the Discovery Centre which is open from Easter to October. Ravenshill is very much a working wood, supporting a wide variety of plants and wildlife. Birds which make this wood their summer home include chiffchaffs, those small warblers which obligingly call their names from high in the canopy, as they establish territories and attract mates. Other breeding birds include nuthatch, treecreepers, woodpeckers and the roding woodcock. Keep an eye open for muntjac deer, foxes and stoats. At the time of writing, the wood and house were up for sale. It's to be hoped that a sympathetic buyer is found, someone who will care for this wood and not turn it into a theme park. (Free to Trust members - otherwise voluntary donations).

We emerge into KNIGHTWICK where St Mary's church dates from 1855. Barely thirty years later, the river Teme, which now glides serenely under the bridge, burst its banks and flooded the church. Today's visitor to the church can appreciate the altar rail kneelers, depicting local wildlife and farming.

A steep road climbs ANKERDINE HILL. Follow the "Badger Trail" from the car park to a viewpoint. If you continue ahead when the Trail turns downhill, you'll come to a dramatic panorama which ranges from a striking end-on view of the Malverns to the blue haze of the Welsh hills, with the

Path in Ravenshill Wood Nature Reserve.

verdant Teme valley and distant hump of Bredon Hill backed by the Cotswold escarpment, filling in the gaps.

Pause awhile at MARTLEY village. St. Peter's chief glory lies in its splendidly preserved wall paintings, which survived the worst ravages of the Victorian restorers. The wall decorations near the altar vividly illustrate how interiors of mediaeval churches once looked.

As we turn towards Shrawley, we pass EASTGROVE COTTAGE GARDEN NURSERY at Sankyns Green. (Open April to October, closed August, Thurs-Sat 2.00-5.00. Admission charge. Tel: 01299 896389). We reach St. Mary's, Shrawley, set apart from the rest of the straggling village. Venture inside to see the chancel arch which leans worryingly, forcing the walls outwards.

Our next destination is SHRAWLEY WOOD. Use the car park behind the New Inn and walk past the post office to enjoy a stroll around this sylvan wonderland. Backing onto the river Severn, this is one of the most magnificent woodlands in the county. The glorious tangle of trees is noted for its small leaved limes and magnificent display of bluebells, as well as its value to wildlife. The Forestry Commission (now called Forest Enterprise) acquired part of the wood in 1959 and immediately instigated its usual policy of planting conifers everywhere. Sanity has returned with the reintroduction of more traditional forestry methods and the conifers are being replaced with broadleaved trees.

Coppiced Limes, Shrawley Wood.

Limes are rare throughout Britain but are, thankfully, still relatively common in Worcestershire. However, even this fine display of limes is but a shadow of its former glory, when the original forest covered large areas of Worcestershire over 5,000 years ago. "Whitewood" is an old name for lime as it produces lengths of white, almost grain free, timber. Coppicing has been practised here for generations as can be seen from the trunks growing from coppiced stools. As well as prolonging a tree's life, coppicing produces changing conditions which are ideal for a variety of animals and birds. With the aid of binoculars, you may see most of the finch, woodpecker and tit families, together with jays and treecreepers. Summer visitors which breed here include chiffchaffs, willow and garden warblers.

Minor lanes, with superb views, meander sleepily through farmland to the picturesque village of WICHENFORD. The 17th century dovecote, of striking black and white timber, deserves special mention. (Open daily, April to October, 9.00-6.00. Small admission charge. National Trust, Tel: 01684 850051)

Our final destination is the woodland at MONKWOOD GREEN. Purchased in 1986 from a private owner by the Worcestershire Wildlife Trust and British Butterfly Conservation Society, it opened to the public the following year. The wood is popular with local walkers who tread several paths radiating from the car park. It's a wonderful place to wander quietly and enjoy delicate flora such as lily of the valley, purple and common

Blossom in Monkwood Nature Reserve, near Monkwood Green village.

spotted orchids. The wood provides an excellent habitat for many species of butterflies, moths and beetles while the birdlife is prolific. Nest boxes are being installed which will benefit bats and dormice as well as birds.

FURTHER EXPLORATION:

The WYRE FOREST is a remarkable place, one of the most valuable and extensive broadleaved woodlands surviving in the Midlands. Once a royal hunting forest, it became an important source of oak for building, charcoal burning and bark for tanning. The forest is a haven for flowers, animals and birds, including grey wagtails, dippers and kingfishers, as well as significant numbers of woodland birds. (Visitor centre, open daily. Tel: 01299 266302).

We have already wandered around UFFMOOR WOOD in TOUR 3. Worth a visit is TIDDESLEY WOOD, also cared for by the Worcestershire Wildlife Trust. Several footpaths traverse the wood and an early morning walk in spring is an unforgettable experience. CHADDESLEY WOOD, near Chaddesley Corbett, a remnant of the Royal Forest of Feckenham, was declared a National Nature Reserve in 1973 in recognition of its value to wildlife.

6. COUNTRY SEATS & COUNTRY GARDENS

Throughout its history Worcestershire has played host to elegant country houses on vast estates. However, many of these opulent mansions have failed to survive intact, crippled by death duties, taxation and burdensome maintenance costs. Conversion into blocks of luxury flats or hotels has been the outcome for many, and few continue as family homes. Of those that do remain, the key to survival is diversification; opening their doors to the public, hosting events and conferences. Elsewhere, the National Trust and English Heritage have rescued many stately homes for us all to enjoy.

Blessed with Worcestershire's fertile soil, generations of gardeners have created beautiful gardens we can all appreciate. Closed during the winter, most houses and gardens are at their colourful best during spring and summer. If you have a choice, avoid peak times such as bank holidays as there's little pleasure in tramping round in a queue, unable to stop and examine anything for fear of the person behind bumping into you.

On our tour, we visit one of the finest stately homes in the area, together with a tranquil garden offering a stunning display of spring and summer flowers.

TOUR 6 – COUNTRY SEATS & COUNTRY GARDENS

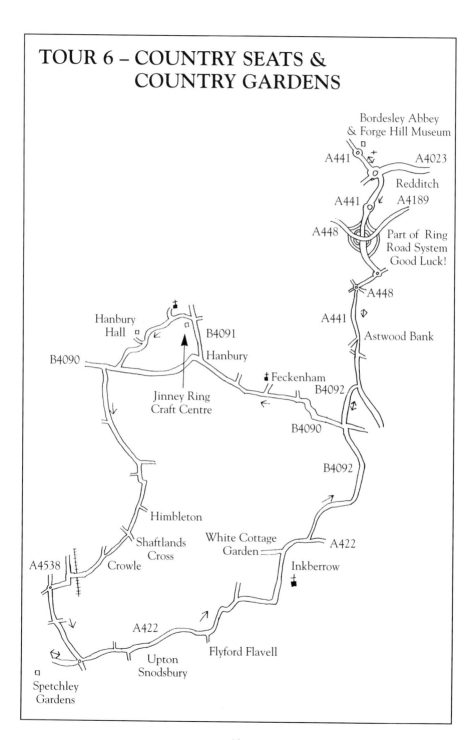

Bordesley Abbey
& Forge Hill Museum

A441   A4023

Redditch

A441   A4189

A448   Part of Ring
            Road System
            Good Luck!

A448

A441   Astwood Bank

Hanbury
Hall   B4091

B4090   Hanbury

            Feckenham

Jinney Ring B4092
Craft Centre

            B4090

            B4092

Himbleton

Shaftlands   White Cottage   A422
Cross   Garden

A4538   Crowle   Inkberrow

A422

            Flyford Flavell

Upton
Snodsbury

Spetchley
Gardens

DIRECTIONS:

Bordesley Abbey lies just off A441 in north Redditch. To continue, take the A441 south out of Redditch (if in doubt on the confusing ring roads, look for signs to Evesham). Drive through Astwood Bank and turn right on B4092 and at staggered crossroads, turn right on B4090. After 5 miles, on a dangerous, blind corner in Hanbury, turn right on B4091. Just past the Jinney Ring Craft Centre, turn left onto minor road, signed Hanbury Hall. Go past turning for Hanbury church and continue to visit Hanbury Hall. Return to minor road and turn right to B4090. Turn right, signed Droitwich and shortly left down another minor road, following signs for Himbleton.

Past the village, go straight across Shaftland Crossroads and through Crowle to go over the railway to T-junction. Turn left to roundabout on A4538. Turn left to another roundabout and turn right on A422 to reach Spetchley Gardens. From the gardens, turn right on A422 through Upton Snodsbury and Inkberrow and turn left on B4092 signed Redditch. Emerge at staggered crossroads, turn left and immediately right to rejoin outward route to Redditch.

APPROX. DISTANCE: 36 miles

RECOMMENDED:

Nevill Arms, New End; Lygon Arms, Feckenham; The Gate Hangs Well, The Country Girl, Craft Centre Restaurant, Hanbury; Tea Shop, Hanbury Hall; Tea Rooms, Spetchley; March Hare Inn, Broughton Hackett; Royal Oak, The Red Lion, Upton Snodsbury; Flyford Arms, Flyford Flavell; Red Hart Inn, The Bourne; Bull's Head Inn, The Old Bull, Inkberrow.

Excavated Bordesley Abbey, Abbey Meadows, near Forge Mill Museum, Redditch.

Jinney Ring Craft Centre, Hanbury.

Before you leave Redditch, pay a visit to BORDESLEY ABBEY. This monastic centre, the seat of Cistercian monks, once stood at the edge of the extensive Feckenham Forest. You can take part in the archaeological digs in progress on the site where an exhibition displays ancient items discovered in the ruins. The abbey stands on the same site as the Forge Mill Museum (see TOUR 2), sharing the same opening hours. Gird up your loins for the road south out of Redditch and concentrate on the road signs. One wrong turn on their baffling ring road system and you could end up in the next county.

Straddling the old salt road is the picturesque village of FECKENHAM which gave its name to the ancient Royal Forest. The satisfying blend of buildings includes "magpie" half timbered, red brick and elegant Georgian. In the churchyard of St. John the Baptist is a horse chestnut tree, still impressive despite being damaged in a storm years ago.

Our next stop is the fascinating JINNEY RING CRAFT CENTRE in Hanbury, an enterprising initiative which has deservedly won many awards. Individual craftsmen, experts in pottery, leather, jewellery, painting, stained glass and wood turning are just a few of the many ancient crafts you can admire. There's also a superb restaurant. (Open all year, Tues-Sat 10.30-5.00, Sun 11.30-5.30. Free admission. Tel: 01527 821272).

A short distance along the road is St. Mary the Virgin Church, halfway between the village and our next port of call, Hanbury Hall. The church

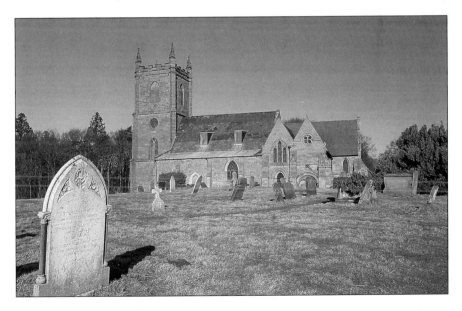

St. Mary the Virgin church, Hanbury.

commands attention from its impressive site high above the surrounding farmland. Superb views, including magnificent sunsets, can be savoured from seats in the churchyard. The exterior is an odd mix of architectural styles but inside you can inspect monuments of the Vernon family including a splendid sculpture by Chantry and a striking east window. Many of the characters from the radio serial, "The Archers" have been married here.

You'll find it hard to tear yourself away from the mouthwatering tea room at HANBURY HALL, but the house and grounds are equally interesting, and less fattening. Cared for by the National Trust, this seat of the Vernon family was completed in 1701. Justly proud of its heritage, the Hall contains

Fountain Gardens, Spetchley Park Gardens.

collections of porcelain, paintings and a magnificent staircase. A walk through ancient parkland leads to an unusual survival, an 18th century ice house in a secluded part of the grounds. (Open April to October, Sat to Weds, 2.00-6.00. Admission charge, free to NT members. Tel: 01527 821214).

We now follow minor roads south to SPETCHLEY PARK GARDENS on the outskirts of Worcester. This enchanting place has long been an inspiration for countless gardeners, and its 30 acres are home to many rare plants, shrubs and trees. Since 1605, Spetchley has been in the possession of the Berkeley family, who also own Berkeley Castle in Gloucestershire. At the beginning of this century, the gardens were substantially extended. All through the summer months, a dazzling array of colour awaits the visitor but April and May are the best months to appreciate the wonderful display of spring flowers. Roses bloom through June and July and the borders are at their best from July to September as the autumn colours provide a last blaze of glory. When you have drunk your fill, a slightly longer walk is possible across the parkland where herds of red and fallow deer roam and a tea room will slake any remaining thirst. (Open April to September, Tues-Fri 11.00-5.00, Sun 2.00-5.00. Admission charge. Tel: 01905 345224)

On our return journey we have the opportunity to turn aside to visit the WHITE COTTAGE GARDEN in Stock Green, north of Inkberrow. This two acre garden boasts a fine display of shrubs and plants as well as a nursery.

Spetchley Park House from Garden Pool, Spetchley Park Gardens.

(Open Easter to November every day except Weds, Thurs and some Sundays. By appointment during August and October. Admission charge. 10.00-5.00. Tel: 01386 792414).

Our final stop is the attractive village of INKBERROW, today better known for its connection with "The Archers" of BBC radio fame. The Old Bull Inn is believed to be the model for the pub in "Ambridge". Despite the busy road running through the heart of the village, Inkberrow has great charm and exudes a trim, well tended atmosphere. The church, festooned with gargoyles and battlements, looms over the village.

FURTHER EXPLORATION:

HARVINGTON HALL is a magnificent, moated Elizabethan manor house noted for its fine collection of wall paintings. Its abundance of priest holes, secret passages, trapdoors and moving panels are a relic from the days when the Hall provided a sanctuary for Catholics fleeing persecution. Four of these ingenious hiding places are believed to be the work of Nicholas Owen, a master builder of such refuges. Nicholas ended his days in the Tower of London following his arrest near Worcester in 1606. (Open March to October, Sun, Tues-Thurs and Bank Holidays. 11.30-5.30. Admission charge. Tel: 01562 777846)

HAGLEY HALL, nestling below the Clent Hills (see TOUR 3), was built for the first Lord Lyttleton by the famous architect, Sanderson Miller. (Open for limited period during summer, dates change each year. Tel: 01562 882408. Admission charge).

STONE HOUSE COTTAGE GARDENS, near Kidderminster is a secluded walled cottage garden with an adjacent nursery. (Open March to October, Weds-Sat 10.00-6.00 plus bank holidays. Admission charge. Tel: 01562 69902).

CROOME LANDSCAPE PARK in the care of the National Trust is now closed for several years for renovations to the lakeside gardens. An exhibition at the church and guided tours on selected dates throughout the summer will explain what the work hopes to achieve. Call the Regional Office (01684 850051) for details. Public footpaths across the estate remain open.

We have visited WITLEY COURT on TOUR 4 and will have the opportunity to see LITTLE MALVERN PRIORY GARDENS on TOUR 7. Many smaller gardens play a part in the NATIONAL GARDENS SCHEME each year and a leaflet with details of their location and opening dates is available from tourist information offices.

7. IF MUSIC BE THE FOOD OF LOVE

(Shakespeare's Twelfth Night)

Worcestershire was the birthplace of one of our greatest composers. Edward Elgar was born at "The Firs" in Upper Broadheath on 2nd June 1857. Two years later, the family moved to Worcester where Elgar attended school. Later, the cathedral became central to his work and until the end of his life, he was associated with the Three Choirs Festival. In 1905, Elgar fittingly received the freedom of the city from the Mayor, his childhood friend, Hubert Leicester.

Elgar's music captures so eloquently the atmosphere and character of a county he called his "beloved country" and it was from the magnificent Malvern Hills that he drew the inspiration for some of his finest work. In all, Elgar lived for over twenty years away from the area, in London, Warwickshire and Sussex but spent his final days in Worcester, where he died on 23rd February 1934. He is buried in a simple grave at St. Wulstan's Church, in the shadow of the Malverns where his spirit still walks abroad.

Our pilgrimage traces places of significance in his life and our first stop, appropriately enough, is his birthplace in Upper Broadheath. Our route partly coincides with the Tourist Board's "Elgar Route" and several handily placed signs will help at difficult junctions. But in case you think I've been busy with a hammer and nails, these signs were erected by the tourist office, not by me!

TOUR 7 – IF MUSIC BE THE FOOD OF LOVE

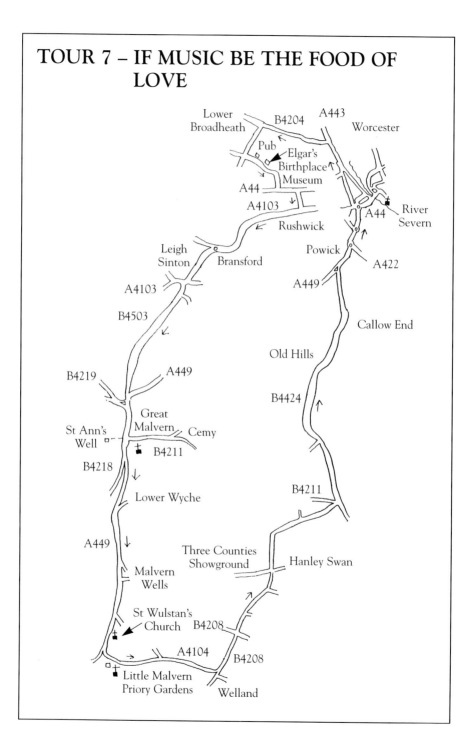

Lower Broadheath

B4204

A443

Worcester

Pub

Elgar's Birthplace Museum

A44

A4103

A44

River Severn

Rushwick

Leigh Sinton

Bransford

Powick

A422

A4103

A449

Callow End

B4503

Old Hills

B4219

A449

B4424

Great Malvern

Cemy

St Ann's Well

B4211

B4218

Lower Wyche

B4211

A449

Three Counties Showground

Hanley Swan

Malvern Wells

St Wulstan's Church

B4208

Little Malvern Priory Gardens

A4104

B4208

Welland

DIRECTIONS:

From Worcester, cross the river on A44, Leominster road, turn right at first roundabout, signed Tenbury. (Note "Elgar Route" sign). Move to left hand lane and at junction turn left, parallel to river. Turn left on B4204 to Lower Broadheath and left to Upper Broadheath to visit birthplace (parking behind pub). Turn left to A44 and left again, and shortly right on minor road to A4103 at Rushwick. (At the time of writing, western bypass is under construction, so road layout and access may change. If in doubt, head for A4103, Hereford Road). Turn right and follow A4103 to Leigh Sinton. Turn left on B4503, follow signs to Great Malvern and emerge onto A449. Turn right and follow signs to Great Malvern town centre. After your visit, return to A449 and turn left, signed Ledbury, through Malvern Wells to St. Wulstan's Church (layby almost opposite).

Turn left on A4104, downhill past Little Malvern Priory and at staggered crossroads in Welland, turn left on B4208. Where B4208 bears left, go straight on, signed Worcester, into Hanley Swan. Turn right and immediately left over staggered crossroads, and after 3 miles reach B4211. Turn right and shortly left onto B4424, through Old Hills and Callow End to Powick. Follow one way system left and then right onto A449 to roundabout. Go straight across and follow signs to Worcester.

APPROX. DISTANCE: 30 miles

RECOMMENDED:

Ample choice in Worcester; The Bell Inn, The Dew Drop Inn, Lower Broadheath; The Plough, Upper Broadheath; Royal Oak, Leigh Sinton; Plenty of choice in Malvern; Railway Inn, Lower Wyche; The Marlbank, A4104; The Swan Inn, Hanley Swan.

Statue of Sir Edward Elgar, Worcester City Centre.

Elgar's connections with WORCESTER make it a natural starting point. Modern reminders of the composer include a statue by the shopping centre, while a stained glass window in the Cathedral, unveiled in Elgar's honour, depicts the Dream of Gerontius.

Our first stop, E L G A R ' S B I R T H P L A C E MUSEUM at Upper Broadheath, has become an important place of pilgrimage for visitors from all over the world. The museum houses a unique collection of photographs, letters, manuscripts and all manner of memorabilia relating to his life and work. For a building so closely associated with the composer, he lived here for only two years. It was his wish that, following his death, the cottage be established as a museum and the Elgar Birthplace Trust was set up by his daughter to maintain this shrine. (Open daily, except Weds, May to September 10.30-6.00, October to April 1.30-4.30. Closed mid Jan to mid Feb. Tel: 01905 333224. The nearby Plough pub offers car parking for museum visitors, as well as meals).

As we head across country, our eyes are irresistibly drawn to the exciting prospect of the MALVERN HILLS. They demand to be climbed. Further north, these hills would merely be pimples but here in the Midlands, they seem like mountains. Rearing impressively to over 1,000 feet, they offer invigorating walking and breathtaking views west to the Welsh borders,

Walker on Pinnacle Hill ridge looking to Worcestershire Beacon, the Malverns.

south to the Cotswolds and east towards Bredon Hill and the Vale of Evesham. One of the main pleasures of the Malverns is their accessibility but that is also part of the problem. On summer weekends and bank holidays, the hills crawl with people and we are in danger of loving them to death. The burden of path maintenance, and providing car parks, falls to the Malvern Hills Conservators who face a difficult task in reconciling the needs of visitors with the protection of this vulnerable landscape. The southern hills, Hollybush and Chase Hill, are much quieter and it's possible to walk in relative seclusion. The Malverns are equally important as a landmark for birds and considerable numbers pause here to rest during the spring and autumn migrations.

GREAT MALVERN, where Elgar lived for a number of years, owes its prosperity to the mineral springs that gush from the hills. The railway increased the town's accessibility and it became a fashionable spa during Victorian times. During the 1840's, success was assured when Drs. Wilson and Gully opened a health centre, where patients were subjected to a regime of dieting, taking the waters, walking on the hills and being wrapped in wet sheets - presumably not all at the same time! Several springs, where you can fill your water bottles, border the road which encircles the hills, and from Great Malvern, a stiff climb leads to St. Ann's Well. As well as sampling the waters, you can enjoy a wonderful view and appreciate how

View over Great Malvern from path to St. Ann's Well, Malvern Hills.

large the town has become, its depressing modern outskirts constantly nibbling away at the surrounding countryside.

Previously, Malvern was a small village centred on a Priory, founded in 1085 as part of a larger Benedictine house. Like so many others, it did not survive the Dissolution, although the church itself was saved when the parishioners bought the building. The £20 price tag was such a large sum of money that it had to be paid in instalments. In later years, this gesture may have been regretted because the maintenance of this grand structure proved far beyond the slender means of the villagers and it became progressively more dilapidated. Renovations eventually became possible, resulting in the Gothic splendour we see today. The west window was given by Richard III and, not to be outdone, his successor, Henry VII, donated the east window. The mediaeval wall and floor tiles, dating from the late 1400's, are considered to be one of the most complete collections in the country. Most were intended for the choir screen although some were originally found on the floor. The floor tiles that remain are 19th century replicas because the originals are too fragile to be walked upon. The setting of this magnificent church, with its small churchyard, is rather curious, squashed in behind the Abbey Hotel. With its ivy-clad walls, this hotel is a particularly colourful sight in autumn.

Nearby, the Abbey Gateway, which houses the Malvern Museum, stands on the site of an earlier wooden entrance to the Priory. You can still see

Grave of Jenny Lind, "The Swedish Nightingale", Great Malvern cemetery.

parts of the original huge timber gateposts although all the original glass was replaced in the 19th century. (Open daily, Easter to end October, 10.30-5.00. Admission charge. Staffed by volunteers. Tel: 01684 567811).

Despite the hordes of visitors, the elegance of Great Malvern, with its tree lined avenues, is undiminished and everywhere you turn, the view is dominated by the Malvern ridge. The railway station has its share of curiosities; see if you can spot the stone dogs on the roof. The colourful Winter Gardens are home to a thriving arts complex, which is in the process of being renovated, courtesy of a grant from the National Lottery. The famous Malvern Festival, devised by Sir Barry Jackson as a tribute to George Bernard Shaw is held here each May.

Several well known figures chose to be buried in Malvern. Peter Mark Roget (he of Thesaurus fame) is buried at West Malvern cemetery and Charles Darwin's daughter lies in the Priory churchyard. The opera singer Jenny Lind, known as "The Swedish Nightingale" used a house at Wynds Point as a summer retreat and she was buried in Great Malvern cemetery. The house, now owned by the Cadbury Trust, is occasionally open around her birthday in October.

We now cross the slopes of the Malverns to pay homage to the Elgar family at their final resting place in ST WULSTAN'S

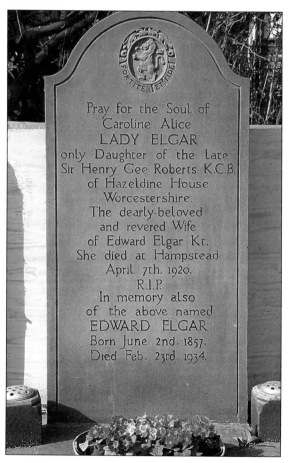

Grave of Sir Edward Elgar, St. Wulstan's church, below Malvern Hills.

CHURCH, Little Malvern. Lady Elgar predeceased Sir Edward in 1920 and their daughter, Carice, was buried next to her parents in 1970.

We pass LITTLE MALVERN PRIORY, whose enchanting gardens and neighbouring church occupies a perfect setting below the Herefordshire Beacon. The priory was originally a monastery dating from 1125, although much of the building was demolished during the Dissolution. The Prior's Hall survived and is now incorporated into Little Malvern Court. (The Gardens are open Weds-Thurs, mid April to mid July, 2.15-4.30. Admission charge. Tel: 01684 892988).

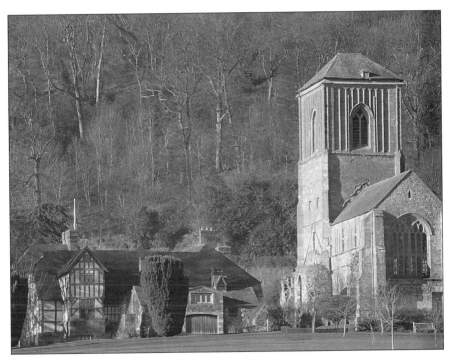

Little Malvern Court & Priory church, Little Malvern.

Our return journey passes close to the Three Counties Showground, which hosts dozens of events throughout the year. The local press or tourist offices can provide dates of the various shows but please remember that traffic can be chaotic at such times. It's hard to resist a final stop in Hanley Swan, grouped timelessly around a duck pond. The road back to Worcester passes the Old Hills, a perfect spot to watch the sun setting over the Malvern Hills.

FURTHER EXPLORATION:

Pick up a leaflet from any TIC if you want to see every site in Worcestershire connected with Elgar. At KEMPSEY, where Elgar lived between 1923 to 1927, he was appointed Master of the King's Musick. BIRCHWOOD LODGE, in Storridge was Elgar's summer cottage from 1898 to 1903 and at LONGDON MARSH, Elgar was inspired to compose "The Apostles" whilst sheltering from a storm in the church porch.

Space precludes citing every famous person linked with Worcestershire but I can't resist mentioning one, in the world of poetry. More commonly associated with Shropshire, A.E. Housman was born in 1859 at Fockbury, just outside Bromsgrove and attended the town's School. A "Housman Trail" leaflet is available from the TIC.

8. CRY HAVOC AND LET SLIP THE DOGS OF WAR
(Shakespeare's Julius Caesar)

The crossed swords battlefield symbols marked on the map outside Worcester and Evesham are mundane reminders of Worcestershire's crucial role in English history. The first city to declare for Charles in the Civil War, Worcester was the last to surrender to the Parliamentarians. The nine years between the Battle of Powick Bridge and the decisive Battle of Worcester saw some of the bloodiest fighting England has ever known. The conflict set neighbour against neighbour, father against son and disease laid waste to the population. This was a time of typhus and the plague.

Many similarities exist between the 13th century Barons' War and the 17th century Civil War. Spurred on by powerful leaders, Simon de Montfort and Oliver Cromwell, the people revolted against a monarchy they were disillusioned with. Both Kings briefly became prisoners but the outcome of the two wars was vastly different. The Barons' War ended in defeat for the rebels at Evesham, while the Civil War saw the monarchy brought to its knees with the death of Charles I and exile for his son. Cromwell's victory became known as his "Crowning Mercy" and led to the establishment of his Protectorate.

The Wars of the Roses, between 1455 and 1485, involved the Houses of York and Lancaster; the white rose and the red. The weak rule of Henry VI sparked a power struggle which saw the crown pass to Edward IV, following the battle at "Bloody Meadow", Tewkesbury, over the border in Gloucestershire. Barely 15 years later, the House of York's reign ended at Bosworth Field with defeat for Richard III.

Our tour, recalling incidents from the Civil War, visits places with a tangible sense of history and we touch on the Barons' War and the Wars of the Roses in "Further Explorations".

TOUR 8 – CRY HAVOC AND LET SLIP THE DOGS OF WAR

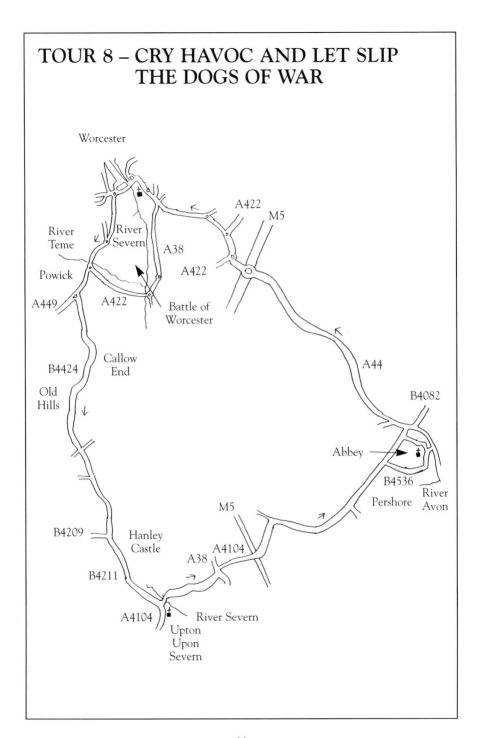

Worcester

A422

M5

River Teme

River Severn

A38

A422

Powick

A422

A449

Battle of Worcester

Callow End

A44

B4424

Old Hills

B4082

Abbey

B4536

Pershore

River Avon

B4209

Hanley Castle

M5

B4211

A4104

A38

A4104

River Severn

Upton Upon Severn

DIRECTIONS:

From Worcester, join A449 (Malvern road), and go straight over the Powick Bridge roundabout. (New bypass under construction, so road layout may change). Turn left in Powick onto B4424 through Callow End to drive alongside the River Severn. The road becomes the B4211 through Hanley Castle to reach Upton upon Severn.

After your visit, join road over bridge on A4104, signed Pershore, and at T-junction, turn left and immediately right, still on A4104. Follow A4104 over M5 to Pershore. After your visit, join A44 to return to Worcester.

APPROX. DISTANCE: *27 miles*

RECOMMENDED:

Plenty of choice in Worcester; The Blue Bell, The Old Bush, Callow End; Ample choice in Upton upon Severn and Pershore; The Jockey, The Gay Dog, Baughton; The Oak Inn, Woodmancote; Railway Inn, Defford Arms, Defford.

The Commandery Civil War Centre.

Known as "The Faithful City" because of its support for the royalist cause, WORCESTER was always strategically important and today's visitor can see many reminders of its bloody past. The effigy of Cromwell, rather ignominiously nailed by his ears over the Guildhall entrance, is a tongue in cheek reminder of where the city's loyalties lay. Looking on, are statues of Charles I and II. The Commandery, Charles II's headquarters before the Battle of Worcester, is now a museum dedicated to the Civil War. If your kids find history dull, bring them here - the displays bring the war vividly to life. (Open Mon-Sat 10.00-5.00, Sun 1.30-5.30. Admission charge. Tel: 01905 355071). King Charles House in New Street is where he took refuge after the battle. Don't miss the beautifully preserved Greyfriars, a National Trust property. (Open April to end October, Weds, Thurs, and Bank Holiday Mon 2.00-5.00. Admission charge, free to members. Tel: 01905 23571).

Effigy of Oliver Cromwell over door of Guildhall, Worcester city centre.

Exploring Worcester is very rewarding, despite some ghastly 60's concrete. Care is also needed in crossing its roads. Although the centre is pedestrianised, some traffic light and bridge crossings are appalling, calling for some nifty footwork. The setting for the cricket ground, on the banks of the Severn with the cathedral as a backdrop, is glorious. A path leads downstream to the confluence of the Severn and Teme and on to Powick Bridge, where, on 23rd September 1642, Prince Rupert's soldiers engaged a party of Cromwell's men. Powick Field is the site of the Battle of Worcester which signalled the end of the Civil War. It's hard to imagine such slaughter in this peaceful spot, with the Teme meandering serenely beneath the bridges at Powick.

Following Charles I's execution in 1649, his son, Charles, was forced into exile. He was crowned in Scotland as Charles II on 1st January 1651 but it was to be many bloody months before he was recognised as England's monarch. At the head of a motley army, Charles crossed the border, intending to meet Welsh reinforcements at Worcester. Estimates differ, between 12 and 16,000, as to the exact number of his soldiers but there is little doubt that his exhausted troops were hopelessly outnumbered by Cromwell's New Model Army of around 30,000. The Parliamentary forces constructed bridges of boats over the Severn and Teme and the final assault began on 3rd September 1651. The Royalist forces were gradually overwhelmed with over half their number taken prisoner. The King abandoned his wretched army and his flight has entered legend as he made his way across country, via the famous Boscobel Oak, to eventual exile in France. It was only after Cromwell's death in 1658 that he returned to reclaim his throne and he was finally crowned in 1660.

Head south to the village of HANLEY CASTLE. The castle, which began life as a royal hunting lodge for King John, fell into ruin during the

View of Worcester Cathedral over site of Battle of Worcester (Civil War).

The Pepperpot, riverside & bridge over river Severn, Upton upon Severn.

time of Henry VII. Our next stop is UPTON UPON SEVERN which developed as a result of its proximity to the river Severn. Flooding still occurs and winter visitors to the riverside pubs would be well advised to bring a canoe. Wander the streets to enjoy the distinguished architecture, particularly the tower, known affectionately as The Pepperpot, which is all that remains of the original church.

The Battle of Upton Bridge took place on 29th August 1651. Charles sent one of his trusted officers, Edward Massey, to Upton with orders to destroy the bridge, the only crossing point on the Severn between Gloucester and Worcester. General Lambert was ordered by Cromwell to drive Massey from Upton and regain possession of the bridge. He dispatched a small band of men across the bridge, who were attacked by the King's army. Amazingly, this small group held out in the church until reinforcements from Lambert arrived. After much bloodshed, the King's army fled and Cromwell regained the town, and, more importantly, secured this key river crossing. It was only a few days later that Charles was soundly defeated at the Battle of Worcester. As you cross the ugly modern bridge, spare a thought for what happened in Upton one dark night over 300 years ago.

After the battle, Cromwell is believed to have visited a house in Church Street, now called Tudor House. Today, the Oliver Cromwell jazz festival is held here every June - I didn't know Ollie was the 17th century's answer to Louis Armstrong!

Continue to PERSHORE, where it's still possible to appreciate the elegant Georgian terraces, despite the traffic. The original settlement developed around the Benedictine Abbey and the first river bridge was built in the 14th century by the monks. It remains the only monastic bridge to survive on the Avon, despite the best efforts of Royalist soldiers, who blew up the central span in a vain attempt to halt Cromwell's forces.

The Abbey, merely a shadow of its former glory, is a wonderful place to wander quietly and soak up the atmosphere. Buy a leaflet and spend time outside where you can see traces of the earlier monastic buildings on the exterior. A line of trees marks the position of the nave pillars and a sturdy flying buttress braces the side of the tower. The monks must have been very careless with matches for their history is littered with disastrous fires. In the 11th century, the abbey was rebuilt after the double whammy of a fire and earthquake, and fire again destroyed part of the structure in the next century. Yet another fire in the late 13th century destroyed not only part of the church but spread to the town, incinerating 40 houses. The interior bears testimony to past glories while a magnificent vaulted roof and individually carved roof bosses reflect the craftsman's skill.

FURTHER EXPLORATION:

The Battle of TEWKESBURY on 4th May 1471 was the culmination of the Wars of the Roses. The Lancastrian army of Henry VI, a prisoner in the Tower at the time, was led by his Queen, Margaret of Anjou. The Yorkist forces were led by Edward Plantagenet, soon to be Edward IV, with his brothers Clarence and Richard, Duke of Gloucester (later the infamous Richard III). The Lancastrian army faltered, fleeing for their lives, only to be cut down by the victorious Yorkists. Henry's son, Edward, was killed, thus ending the Lancastrian line. A hunted Queen Margaret sought refuge at nearby Bushley Green. A battlefield trail leaflet is available from the tourist office. The Norman abbey, a building of grace and beauty, together with the riverside meadows and striking mill building all add to the charm of this historic town.

EVESHAM (see TOUR 10) saw the end of the Barons' War in 1265 when the armies of the Earl of Leicester, Simon de Montfort and the reigning monarch, Henry III, met on Greenhill. The war began just 50 years after Magna Carta, when the Barons, supported by the church, attempted to curb royal power. A council was established under the leadership of de Montfort, the King's brother-in-law, with the power to control the King's actions. Not unnaturally, this was resisted by Henry III and in 1264, civil war broke out. Emergency meetings, or parliaments as they became known, were attended by the barons, clergy, knights and burgesses from each shire, and it was hoped a lasting agreement would be reached. Some hope, if they were anything like our Westminster "kindergarten". Support for the Earl's cause began to crumble and Henry's son, Edward, assembled a royal army and in 1265, marched to Evesham. Trapped between Edward's army in front and the river behind, Simon is believed to have said "Now God have mercy on our souls, for our bodies are our enemies". Simon, his son Henry, and many barons were killed and Simon's mutilated body was eventually buried secretly by the monks. His memorial in Abbey Park stands on the old site of the high altar. It is ironic that when Edward eventually became King he continued the reform of royal power, recognising that cooperation was more effective than the coercion of resentful subjects. As we have seen, it would take a few more centuries and a civil war before those reforms formed the basis of our current system of government. An obelisk, the Leicester Tower, erected on the battlefield in de Montfort's memory stands on private land. One place you can visit is the Almonry, a striking building and the former home of the Abbey Almoner. A model of the battle can be seen in the Heritage Centre. (Open March to November, Tues, Thurs-Sat 10.00-5.00, Sun 2.00-5.00. Tel: 01386 446944).

Cottages, Elmley Castle, near Bredon Hill

9. HOME SWEET HOME
(J.H. Payne)

Worcestershire's dominant black and white half timbered building style owes its existence to the ready availability of wood from the once extensive native woodland. The county boasts its fair share of Georgian and Victorian architecture along with 20th century functional red brick. We now turn our sights to some of the most attractive villages in south Worcestershire, near the border with Gloucestershire where the influence of the Cotswold golden stone is strongly felt.

The sudden upthrust of Bredon Hill forms a physical barrier between Worcestershire and the Cotswolds, which is reflected in the contrasting architecture to be found in its necklace of villages. Bredon village marks a change in style to the more familiar Worcestershire half-timber; Ashton under Hill, Great and Little Comberton and Elmley Castle all contain splendid examples of this striking architecture. On the southern slopes of Bredon Hill, the villages of Conderton, Beckford, Overbury and Kemerton have their architectural heart firmly rooted in the Cotswolds. Although we stay entirely in Worcestershire on our route, the villages of warm, honey coloured stone, stone mullions and pointed gables are as lovely as any you'll find in deepest Gloucestershire.

TOUR 9 – HOME SWEET HOME

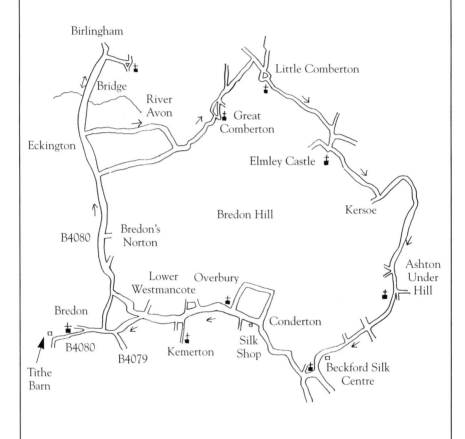

Birlingham

Bridge

River
Avon

Little Comberton

Great
Comberton

Eckington

Elmley Castle

Bredon Hill

Kersoe

B4080

Bredon's
Norton

Lower
Westmancote

Overbury

Ashton
Under
Hill

Bredon

Conderton

B4080

B4079

Kemerton

Silk
Shop

Beckford Silk
Centre

Tithe
Barn

DIRECTIONS:

From Bredon village, head north on B4080 for nearly 3 miles to Eckington. Continue ahead over Eckington Bridge, and take first right to Birlingham. Return over Eckington bridge and turn left, signed The Combertons. Road eventually swings right to T-junction. Turn left to Great Comberton. Continue through village, following signs for Little Comberton. At a junction, turn right into village. Keep ahead through Little Comberton and follow minor road to Elmley Castle. Ignore two left turns to reach village, bear right up main street and opposite Queen Elizabeth pub, turn left down awkward narrow lane, signed Kersoe. The lane widens and after a mile, bends left, past turning to Kersoe.

Continue for almost 2 miles to Ashton under Hill. Drive through village, ignoring side turnings to pass church. Follow minor road for 2 miles to Beckford and at T-junction, turn right passing church. Follow winding road to Conderton and bear left to Overbury. Keep ahead through village, past church and alongside parkland to reach Kemerton. Ignore left turns, continue through Lower Westmancote and bear left to return to Bredon.

APPROX. DISTANCE: 21 miles

RECOMMENDED:

The Fox and Hounds, Bredon; The Anchor Inn, The Bell Inn, Eckington; Queen Elizabeth, Elmley Castle; The Star Inn, Ashton under Hill; Silk Centre Coffee Shop, The Beckford Inn, Beckford; The Yew Tree, Elaine Rippon Coffee Shop & Silk Centre, Conderton; The Crown, Kemerton.

Thatched cottage, Bredon.

We begin our journey in BREDON, a village of considerable size, whose charming mix of styles reflects the community's long history. St. Giles Church boasts a striking spire which towers over the village but its chief glory lies inside, with fine 14th century stained glass in the chancel window. The stone monuments are worthy of inspection, especially that of Sir Giles Reed, who lies with his wife in a gaudy Jacobean tomb. Next door, on top of the Rectory roof, are two remarkable stone figures on horseback; use binoculars or a long camera lens to see them in detail. They are said to represent Charles II and Oliver Cromwell and are, understandably enough, at opposite ends of the roof. The National Trust 14th century Tithe Barn is a distinctive building, 132 feet long with an unusual stone chimney cowling. (Open April to end November, Weds, Thurs and weekends. 10.00-6.00. Admission fee, free to members. Tel: 01684 850051).

We head north, passing through Eckington to BIRLINGHAM, whose churchyard has a truly beautiful display of spring flowers, with a gleaming white carpet of snowdrops. Return over Eckington bridge and follow narrow roads east, enjoying splendid views towards BREDON HILL. Rising abruptly from the surrounding plain, its very isolation proved ideal for our ancestors who erected an ancient fort on the summit. Also on the plateau

Gateway framing St. James church, Birlingham village, nr. Bredon Hill.

and clearly visible from the road, is a curious structure, called Parson's Folly which, on closer inspection, leans drunkenly. Built by Mr Parsons of Kemerton in the 18th century, the tower is now festooned with modern aerials. Paths from every satellite village ascend the hill and you'll find the superb views ample reward for all the effort.

Parson's Folly, summit of Bredon Hill.

GREAT COMBERTON looks towards Worcester, and its architecture of half timbered cottages, mixed with brick, reflects the county's traditional style. St. Michael and All Angels Church boasts an imposing tower and a simple white washed interior overlooked by a splendid nave roof.

We soon reach the cottages of LITTLE COMBERTON, loosely grouped alongside the road. The history of St. Peter's can be traced back to the 12th century and many of the original features remain, including a wall painting. Roman pottery and coins indicate an even richer history while sea water shells are a relic of the time when much of England was on the sea bed, the hills rising as islands in a vast ocean. The churchyard is graced by a majestic display of spring flowers and marvellous views to Bredon Hill can be enjoyed from the seat at the rear of the church.

Carry on to ELMLEY CASTLE, a delightful village with a picturesque blend of stone houses, liberally dotted with timber framed buildings. A stream burbles alongside the pavements in the tree-lined main street. Inside St. Mary's Church, alabaster monuments to the Coventry family and the

Cottages, Elmley Castle.

Animal stone carving, porch, St. Mary's church, Elmley Castle.

grandiose tomb of the Earl of Coventry are worthy of inspection. The font is a gem with eight sides, all individually carved - even the pedestal has carved dragons. Look especially for the Tudor rose and Prince of Wales plumes. Inside the porch are stone carvings of animals and in the churchyard, the sundials are claimed to be only eight minutes behind GMT. The castle which gave Elmley its name was already in ruins by the 1400's. A model of how the castle once looked stands inside the church alongside an interesting display of the castle's history by local schoolchildren. A favourite Sunday afternoon pastime is to watch cricket on the green and enjoy a drink from one of the popular pubs.

As we turn the corner around Bredon Hill and start to catch glimpses of the distant Cotswold escarpment, this change is reflected in ASHTON UNDER HILL. The charm of the village is enhanced by the harmonious jumble of black and white, red brick and occasional Cotswold stone dwelling. It's heartening to see a surviving village school, despite the ugliness of its buildings. The Norman church is dedicated to St. Barbara, the patron saint of miners, gunners and blacksmiths, an odd commemoration for a place of worship. In spring, the approach path from the lychgate leads through a display of snowdrops and daffodils. Outside the lychgate is a "weeping cross", dating from the 15th century when villagers were compelled to atone for their sins.

Golden stone cottages characterise the village of BECKFORD as we move further round the hill. The Jacobean Hall stands on the site of a 12th century Augustinian priory and over the church doorway is a fantastic tympanum with an array of animal and human heads. The Beckford Silk centre carries out silk printing for clients as diverse as the National Trust and Buckingham Palace. (Open all year, Mon to Sat 9.00-5.30. Tel: 01386 881507).

We pass through the hamlet of CONDERTON, characterised by Cotswold stone, which houses a pottery centre and silk shop, where silk is handpainted. As we arrive at the enchanting village of OVERBURY, we are truly in Cotswold country, with magnificent views towards Gloucestershire. The honey coloured cottages have a trim, neat appearance and the display of garden flowers and trees make a particularly charming picture. Outside St. Faith's church, an unusual timbered lychgate shelters the village war memorial. In the churchyard, magnolia and cherry trees are a colourful sight in spring and the memorial garden is peaceful and moving. The stream, its banks clothed in delicate spring flowers, is a delightful feature of the churchyard and adds to the overall impression of harmony. But Overbury

Pond in lane in front of St. Faith's church, Overbury village, on slopes of Bredon Hill.

was not always so tranquil. The stream, which runs from the top of the village to form a pond at the bottom of the lane, once provided the power for at least six mills, producing silk, flour, grist and paper. Elegantly Georgian, Overbury Court rose from the ashes of the old house which burnt down in the 1730's. Many houses are still owned by the Overbury Estate which provides a great deal of local employment.

Our final stop is leafy KEMERTON, a place of charm and distinction, full of fine dwellings in Cotswold stone. The Priory is a small garden with many unusual plants and shrubs. (Open June-Sept, Thurs afternoons plus some Sundays. Admission charge. Tel: 01386 725258). As we return to Bredon and catch sight of the Malverns, we are reminded that we have remained in Worcestershire for the entire Tour, despite the architectural distance we have travelled.

FURTHER EXPLORATION:

Every village in Worcestershire has something of interest and many are as outstandingly beautiful as the ones on this Tour. Here are two of my favourites. OMBERSLEY is a charming place with an enclave of black and white, timber framed houses. The King's Arms may have given refuge to Charles II in his flight from defeat at Worcester and on the small green is a rare, hollowed out Plague Stone. During the Black Death, this stone was placed there to deposit food for the suffering villagers and to warn travellers to avoid it, literally, like the plague.

CHADDESLEY CORBETT'S main street is an exquisite black and white chessboard. The church dedication to St. Cassian is unique. You can buy booklets from the church on the history of both the church and the village.

10. BLOSSOM BY BLOSSOM THE SPRING BEGINS
(Algernon Charles Swinburne)

In spring, the Vale of Evesham undergoes a stunning transformation. The plum and apple orchards burst into life and the swathes of colour from the heavily laden blossom are outstandingly beautiful. The rich soil has given rise to a prolific fruit and vegetable industry and you'll find many farm shops and nurseries offering produce for sale.

Since the middle ages, apples and pears have been grown to make cider and perry (a drink made from fermented pear juice). By the 19th century, fruit growing was enormously successful. Many new varieties were introduced, including the Pershore plum, found in Tyddesley Wood in 1833. Around 3,000 acres are still devoted to orchards but this is shrinking each year, as supermarket chains dictate our eating habits and import most of our fruit and vegetables from abroad. Many orchards have disappeared under housing or roads - presumably tarmac is more profitable than fruit growing. The new bypass near Evesham recently swallowed yet more acres.

Cherry trees are no longer popular, although you may still see a few varieties. Plum varieties still grown include Victoria and Pershore Purple, along with exotic strains such as Yellow Egg, Early Rivers' Seedling, Heron, Monarch and Marjorie's Seedling. Apples grown include Cox's, Bramley, Howgate Wonder, Discovery and Worcester Pearmain. Wonderful names which, if left to Brussels, would probably be changed to the Euro plum and the Euro apple.

The blossom is very dependent on the weather and is often at its best for only a short time, any time between the end of March and the middle of May. White Plum and Damson blossom are the first to appear, followed by white and pink apple blossom about ten days later. But even if you miss the blossom, a tour of the villages around Evesham makes a fascinating day out.

TOUR 10 – BLOSSOM BY BLOSSOM THE SPRING BEGINS

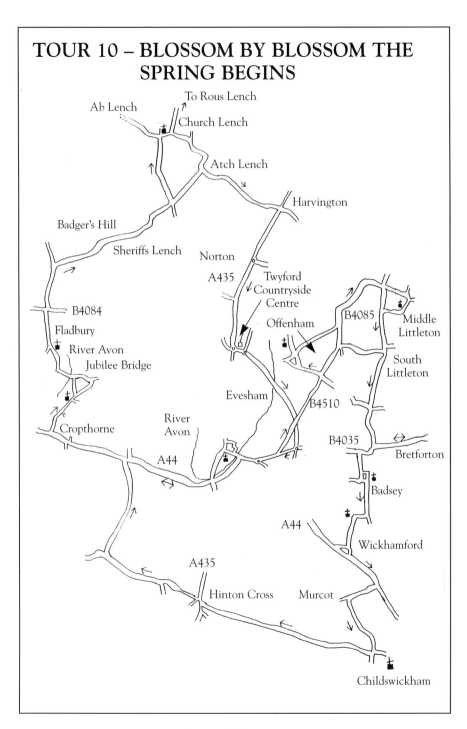

Ab Lench

To Rous Lench

Church Lench

Atch Lench

Harvington

Badger's Hill

Sheriffs Lench

Norton

A435

Twyford
Countryside
Centre

B4085

Middle
Littleton

Offenham

B4084

Fladbury

River Avon
Jubilee Bridge

South
Littleton

Evesham

B4510

Cropthorne

River
Avon

B4035

Bretforton

A44

Badsey

A44

Wickhamford

A435

Hinton Cross

Murcot

Childswickham

DIRECTIONS:

Join A44 from Evesham heading west and after 4 miles, turn right to Cropthorne. Pass the church and turn left. Left again at T-junction over Jubilee Bridge to Fladbury. Go past church to T-junction with B4084. Turn right and immediately left onto minor road, signed The Lenches. After a mile, turn right through Badger's Hill, Sheriff's Lench and at crossroads, turn left to Church Lench. In village, road bends right by church. Ignore left turns, go through Atch Lench and bend left to Harvington. Turn right on A435, go straight over roundabout through Norton and at another roundabout, go left onto bypass past Twyford Countryside Centre. Return to roundabout, go left and at next roundabout, right onto B4035, signed Evesham.

Turn right onto B4510, signed Offenham, over bypass, and turn left to Offenham. Rejoin B4510 and turn left to swing right by riverside to B4085 crossroads. Turn right and first left to Middle Littleton. Return to junction and turn left, down B4085 through South Littleton and with B4035, turn left to Bretforton. Return down B4035 and turn left to Badsey. Zig-zag through Badsey, then turn right through Wickhamford. At T-junction, turn left and left again on A44. Take first right on minor road, signed Murcot. Follow signs to Childswickham and turn right at crossroads, signed Evesham, to reach A435 at Hinton Cross. Go straight over and after 2 miles, turn right to A44 where a right turn leads to Evesham.

APPROX. DISTANCE: 34 miles

RECOMMENDED:

Plenty of choice in Evesham; The Chequers Inn, Anchor Inn, Fladbury; Norton Grange, A435; Twyford Country Centre café; The Bridge, Fish & Anchor, Offenham; King Edward VII, South Littleton; The Wheatsheaf Inn, The Fleece, Bretforton; Sandys Arms, Wickhamford; Childswickham Inn, Childswickham.

EVESHAM, a bustling market town, lies at the heart of Worcestershire's market gardening area. Visitors are attracted to Evesham for its glorious riverside meadows and parkland, as well as the opportunity to mess about on boats. No two buildings are alike; years of restoration and extensions have left a hotch-potch of architectural styles. In the Market Place is a real architectural puzzle - the building known as the Round House is in fact completely square. We have covered Evesham's connections with the Barons' War on Tour 8.

Evesham was once dominated by a magnificent, wealthy Abbey. Built around 700 AD by Egwin, Bishop of Worcester, it was one of the largest in the country. Imagine a structure as huge as Gloucester Cathedral sited high above the river Avon. You can see a model of the Abbey in the Almonry museum but the only tangible reminder of this grandeur stands in Abbey Park in the shape of the Bell Tower, completed in 1533, only a few years before the Dissolution. Near the tower, the churches of All Saints and St. Lawrence are unusual neighbours in the same churchyard. St. Lawrence, now in the care of the Redundant Churches Trust, is a peaceful, simple place. In All Saints, you can admire the beauty of the splendid Lichfield chantry, which holds the tomb of the last Abbot.

We head west to CROPTHORNE, an attractive village with fine black and white cottages where, each May, the villagers open their colourful

Berries on doorway, St. Michael's church, Cropthorne, nr Evesham.

gardens to visitors. A rare survivor in St. Michael's Church is the head of a Saxon cross, adorned with images of birds and beasts, which was found embedded in the sanctuary wall. The church houses a lifelike memorial to Elizabeth and Francis Dingley and their amazing 19 children. No wonder she looks tired!

A car park and picnic area lies alongside the River Avon by Jubilee Bridge, which was built in 1887. Until that time, it was only possible to ford the river in favourable conditions. Rising as a humble stream in Naseby, the Avon gathers pace through Warwickshire passing such famous places as Warwick and Stratford upon Avon before entering Worcestershire at Cleeve Prior. Swinging in great loops around Bredon Hill, the river eventually swells the waters of the Severn at Tewkesbury.

FLADBURY overlooks the Avon and it is to this great waterway that the picturesque village owes its development. The 16th century mill was in use until 1930 and a ferry once linked both banks of the river. Craycombe House was at one time the home of the novelist Francis Brett Young. In St. John the Baptist's Church is a glass panel believed to originate from Evesham Abbey. Of special interest are the shields of Henry III and Simon de Montfort, as well as memorial brasses to John Throckmorton and his wife. The Throckmortons are better known as the owners of Coughton Court in Warwickshire.

War memorial & cottages, Fladbury, nr Evesham.

As you drive into open country, acres of spectacular blossom dominate the landscape. We weave through places of great charm, known collectively as The Lenches which include the quaint hamlets of Ab Lench, Atch Lench and Sheriffs Lench. CHURCH LENCH, the largest, boasts beautiful cottages, including the miniature delight of Toy Cottage in Malt House Lane. In ROUS LENCH there is an unusual pillar box on a stone plinth with timbered eaves. The magnificent Norman church of St. Peter's contains notable monuments from every period and the altar triptych is worthy of inspection. I'm afraid you won't find any pubs; this is a legacy of the original landowners who would not allow any alehouses on their estates.

After passing through Harvington, you have the opportunity to visit TWYFORD COUNTRYSIDE CENTRE, which offers a wide range of garden equipment, plants, trees and shrubs for sale. A farm shop, antiques centre, café, crafts centre and falconry cater for most interests and from the picnic area you can follow footpaths along the river. (Open daily. 9.00-6.00 in summer. 9.00-5.00 in winter. Tel: 01386 442278).

After flirting with the outskirts of Evesham, we reach OFFENHAM. A group of picturesque, 15th century cottages, huddled together under one long piece of thatch, are called, rather

Blossoms, Twyford Countryside Centre, nr Evesham.

obviously, Long Thatch. The maypole nearby is a rare feature of any village today. This one has been here only since 1987 although the tradition of a maypole on this site dates back to 1660. James Myatt, a villager, developed new varieties of fruit and vegetables and both his name and that of the village can be found in current seed catalogues. In the churchyard of St. Mary and St. Milburgh's stands a 14th century stone turret, minus its bell and on the tower are gruesome, if rather worn, gargoyles.

It's worth pausing at MIDDLE LITTLETON to visit the famous 140 foot long Tithe Barn, now in the care of the National Trust. (Open daily, April to end Oct, 9.00-5.00. Admission charge except to members. Tel: 01684 850051). Also worth a short detour is The Fleece Inn, BRETFORTON. The only pub in the care of the National Trust, this half timbered building was originally a farmhouse. The interior is largely unchanged and Witches' Marks can be found in the Pewter Room and Brewhouse. These circles, chalked on the hearth, were supposed to prevent witches coming down the chimney. (Open normal pub hours to everyone except witches! Tel: 01386 831173). Inside St. Leonard's Church, the pillar capitals are worth examining. The carving of a dragon caught in the act of swallowing St. Margaret is as much a tribute to the craftman's sense of humour as his skill. Margaret, far from giving in to her fate, has used her cross to cut a hole in the dragon's side and is struggling to crawl out.

Our next stop is BADSEY where St. James Church is the focal point of the community. The older half of the village lines a pleasant main street, while an area of new housing lies further north. The discovery of Roman coins and pottery indicate Badsey's venerable history.

WICKHAMFORD, a village of half timbered buildings, is probably more familiar to motorists as the site of fruit and vegetable stalls during the summer. Of equal interest is the 13th century St. John the Baptist Church with its beautiful three decker pulpit. An intriguing floor slab memorial is dedicated to a distant relative of George Washington, Penelope, whose coat of arms bears two bars and three stars, which may have inspired the American flag.

Our final stop is at CHILDSWICKHAM, clustered around a village green and a memorial cross. The Norman church of St. Mary the Virgin has an unusual font and a towering 15th century spire. You can visit the Barnfield Cider and Wine Mill and Museum. (Open summer 9.30-8.00, winter 9.30-5.00. Free admission. Tel: 01386 853145). We return to Evesham via roads which pass through yet more colourful orchards.

FURTHER EXPLORATION:

The Teme valley is another prominent centre for fruit growing and if you follow Tour 4, you will see many delightful orchards, nestling in hidden valleys. North of Malvern, the area around Storridge and Leigh Sinton is equally productive.

TOURIST INFORMATION CENTRES IN WORCESTERSHIRE:

BEWDLEY
Load Street
Tel: 01299 404740

BROMSGROVE
47/49 Worcester Road
Tel: 01527 31809

DROITWICH SPA
Droitwich Heritage Centre,
Heritage Way
Tel: 01905 774312

EVESHAM
The Almonry Museum,
Abbey Gate
Tel: 01386 446944

KIDDERMINSTER*
Severn Valley Railway,
Comberton Hill
Tel: 01562 829400

MALVERN
The Winter Gardens,
Grange Road
Tel: 01684 892289

PERSHORE
High Street
Tel: 01386 554262

REDDITCH
Civic Square, Alcester Street
Tel: 01527 60806

UPTON UPON SEVERN*
The Pepperpot, Church Street
Tel: 01684 594200

WORCESTER
The Guildhall, High Street
Tel: 01905 726311

*Seasonal opening only.

ACKNOWLEDGEMENTS

Mr Johnson of Great Witley church committee for permission to photograph the church interior.

English Heritage for the loan of the transparency of Witley Court.

Rod Lövgreen for help with the chapter on Elgar and information about Malvern.

My husband, Rex, for accompanying me on all my trips, carrying the camera equipment and proof reading my many typing errors.

S.B. Publications publish a wide range of local interest books. For a catalogue please write (enclosing S.A.E.) to:- S.B. Publications, c/o 19 Grove Road, Seaford, East Sussex BN25 1TP.